Making Your Net *Work* – Networlding
(Apex Award Winner

OVERVIEW AND WELCOME!

Welcome to Making Your *NetWork* Meets *Networlding*. This is a collaboration of dedicated thought leaders across the country and the world that:
- Share in the belief that anything is possible,
- Strive to make a positive difference in the lives of others, and
- Do good while doing well.

Networlding is the art and science of making meaningful connections and leveraging those connections in new and powerful ways. Our best practices are designed to help your organization master the intersection of traditional networking and social media.

Our proven content will allow your best assets – your people – to learn the Networlding process, creating and leveraging a network of support for both short term and long-term goals – ultimately transforming your business.

The creation of this training course is an example of Networlding in action: Values, Collaboration and Leadership.

Our sincere hope that your organization finds value in this course, and applies its principles for the greatest success. It is in true alignment with the mission of Networlding, "creating the greatest good for the greatest number."

Billy Dexter and Melissa G Wilson

net(worlding   VALUES.COLLABORATION.LEADERSHIP.

TABLE OF CONTENTS

Networlding

VALUES. COLLABORATION. LEADERSHIP.

OVERVIEW

Each step contains an agenda, objectives, lessons, and exercises. There are several instructional cues in this guide to help you lead a Networlding course.

SCRIPT: Each step contains scripts to help you guide the class. As you become more familiar with the content, you may want to create your own scripts. Scripts cover key concepts and help with the course flow.

FACILITATOR NOTE: Facilitator notes contain additional support for content, activities, and class management. Be sure to familiarize yourself with them.

DIRECTIONS FOR FACILITATOR: Each exercise contains facilitator directions to help with proper setup and delivery.

DEBRIEF: Exercises and discussions contain a debrief, helping you guide the class uncover conclusions and better apply the content.

CLOSING DISCUSSION: This will allow you to conclude a step and properly setup the next Networlding step.

NOTES

Add any notes here.

INTRODUCTION TO NETWORLDING

The Facilitator Guide is designed as a resource to help you facilitate groups through the seven steps of the Networlding methodology. To support your work, you will find suggested timelines, scripts, notes, activities, and dialogue points along the way. You are welcome to tailor these as you see fit to create the best experience for your audience or circle group.

For this segment, you may want a flip chart or whiteboard. Participants have a corresponding guide to follow along. Familiarize yourself with the participant guide.

AGENDA

Customize the agenda timing as needed; optionally combine Introduction and Step 1.

TIME	ACTION	OBJECTIVE
10 minutes	Welcome and Logistics	Communicate objectives
10 minutes	Icebreaker	Establish early rapport; demonstrate Emotional Exchange Model
5 minutes	Lesson 1: Working Your Net	Introduce the core ideas
10 – 20 minutes	Lesson 2: Distinguishing Relational and Transactional Approaches	Describe differences between "networking" and "Networlding":
15 – 20 minutes	Lesson 3: Why Do People Dislike Networking?	Highlight some commonly-held negative views of networking
15 – 20 minutes	Lesson 4: Networking vs. Networlding – Why Does It Matter?	Elicit group perspectives
20 – 30 minutes	Lesson 5: Take the Networlding Assessment	Give participants a general idea of their current level of Networlding expertise

OBJECTIVES

The objectives for the Introduction:
- Compare our understanding of networking and Networlding and why Networlding matters today
- Discover the values that will become our foundation in creating Networlding relationships
- Understand our current level of Networlding expertise, and what we can do to improve our Networlding capabilities

Net(worlding

VALUES. COLLABORATION. LEADERSHIP.

WELCOME AND LOGISTICS

(10 MINUTES)

Facilitator creates a script to describe the following:
- What Networlding means to him/her
- How he/she came to be there facilitating the course
- Objectives for the overall course and the day's session
- Any pertinent logistical information

The facilitator should be working to:
- Establish rapport with the participants early on
- Create a safe environment for sharing information, ideas, goals, and dreams
- Model Networlding values and the Support Exchange Model

SCRIPT: [The following is a sample. Be sure to create your own.]

Welcome to Making Your Net *Work* and *Networlding*.

As we move through the world building relationships, so many of us realize that they don't like the word "networking." Why? It carries negative connotations for us, and especially as women.

Networlding is different though as it offers a way for us to truly collaborate with those who have the traits we value - for the good of all involved. It's a way for us to use our natural strengths—and be ourselves in the process. And as we move through this process, you'll hopefully develop your own view of Networlding.

So as we move through this session, there are a couple of objectives we are looking to accomplish:
- Compare our understanding of Networlding and why it matters today
- Understand our current level of Networlding expertise, and what we can do to improve our Networlding capabilities
- Discover the values that will become our foundation in creating Networlding relationships

There are a couple of important things to keep in mind as we work together:
- Your stories, ideas, and knowledge are important. Please know that it's safe to share them in this environment
- We all have many experiences that brought us here today, so let's learn from one another.
- To make the most of this course you need to apply what you learn – to share. It's the only way to retain and improve your knowledge.
- Develop rapport and chemistry first before discussing leads and referrals.
- Be an active listener, listening more than you talk. Learn about the individual first so that you may find ways to support them.

ICEBREAKER

(10 MINUTES)

FACILITATOR NOTE: Icebreaker assumes people in class don't know one another. If that's not the case, substitute another icebreaker/activity suitable to the class.

FACILITATOR NOTE: This activity will help establish early rapport. Notice that there are two "phases" to this introduction exercise. In the first phase, the participants are simply sharing some basic facts. In the second phase, they are going a bit deeper and sharing some more personal information and a point of commonality. This second phase demonstrates Emotional Support in the exchange model.

SCRIPT: We're going to get started with some conversation. At your tables, share the following information:
- Introduce yourself (keep it brief)
- One thing you'd like to take away from the workshop

Now add the following information:
- Share one interesting fact about yourself.
- Share what always makes you laugh or brings a smile to your face.
- Share what you love to do, or would love to do more of in your life.
- Once you've done that, as a group identify one thing you all have in common at the table. An example might be that you all have children.

You'll have about 5 minutes to complete the activity before we come back together as a group.

DEBRIEF: In the interest of time, ask two questions:
1. Ask which "phase" of the introduction they related to in a better way.
2. Ask each table to share the one thing they all have in common. Tie icebreaker to the Support Exchange Model focused on emotional support.

SCRIPT: We've gone around the room and shared information and found some commonalities. Those are the beginnings of building Networlding relationships that incorporate the best strategies and tactics embedded in "Making Your Net *Work*.. What you've done is establish the beginnings of the Networlding Support Exchange Model – the seven levels of support that will help you build relationships that grow and benefit all parties involved when two people exchange wisely. When this happens, as we've discovered from interviewing hundreds of the best networkers in the world: "anything is possible."

LESSON 1 - WORKING YOUR NET

(5 MINUTES)

Insight from **Making Your Net *Work***
Chapter 2: Working Your Net

SCRIPT: We use the metaphor of a "net" to explore the principles of creating a successful network. We capitalized the *N* in net and the *W* in work in Net*Work*ing to emphasize this idea. If you visualize your own net you'll see how you've used it to build one significant connection after another. It's important to note the value of every connecting point in your network.

In this course I'll give you an insider's view of networking effectively. How? By showing you both the *art* and the *science* of the process, and by teaching you how to differentiate between the two. I'll also show you how to balance the art and the science to get the most out of every networking situation and to help you develop a significant and rewarding career path.

This course comes out of two decades of focus on the *science* of building successful networks. There is also *art*—creative and intuitive—something we do naturally. We can be very intentional (scientific) when building networks, and *strategic* without being manipulative.

FACILITATOR NOTE: The Participant Guidebook has fill-in-the-blank prompts for capturing this next set of bullet points.

What I mean by *strategic* is that we are *awake in our networks*. That means we consciously build our connections by:
- Making time to meet new people.
- Listening deeply and asking probing questions.
- Looking for connection points, whether commonalities, mutual interests, or people we have in common. Creating this shared foundation helps us build the relationships.
- Focusing on giving first. This usually starts with asking, "How can I help you?" This approach, along with other strategies and tactics, has brought us both successful careers and fulfilling professional and personal friendships.
- Being passionate about helping people grow in their careers and businesses by managing the nuances of building their networks.

FACILITATOR NOTE: Ask participants what questions people often have about networking, and what questions they have. Capture the questions on a flipchart. Don't attempt to answer them now. Instead, assure participants that these questions will be addressed through the process they will engage in during the seminar.

Some typical questions include:
- What is a network?
- Why do I hate networking?
- Can I change my attitude?
- Isn't this mostly a big time waster?
- What is my philosophy as to how I should network?
- Who should I bring into my network?
- Where should I network?
- What types of organizations or associations should I join?
- How can I network most effectively?
- How big should I grow my network?
- How can I network well while keeping my values?
- What types of people are the best networking partners?
- I don't know a lot of powerful people or have big-name connections—does that matter?
- Won't giving away my connections hurt my business?

SCRIPT: As you can tell, you're not alone in having questions about networking. Especially in a world centered around social media, networking can be very confusing. Throughout this course we'll share experiences and insights to resolve these kinds of questions.

Each of us has many networks. We walk in and out of our different networks every day. Understanding the many networks in your daily life is the first step in your journey to optimize your networking.

We all network differently, so don't worry if your comfort level is higher or lower than someone else's. It takes practice. Making your net *work* doesn't happen overnight, and there is no silver bullet. We'll help you develop a strategy and a set of tactics that will work best for you. As with any skill set, knowing your goals and personality, your social style, and your current strengths, is critical.

Networking effectively changed my perception of myself and my career path, but most of all, it changed my life for the better. I would never have met so many great people had I not made a commitment to strategic networking as a way of growing my career and improving my life and the lives of so many others.

LESSON 2 - DISTINGUISHING RELATIONAL AND TRANSACTIONAL APPROACHES

(10-20 minutes)

SCRIPT: This brings us to Lesson 2: defining networking vs. Networlding - and why it matters. By "network" we mean conventional approaches to networking – the way most people engage in networking. "Networlding" denotes the specific process we will cover in this course that will lead to the kinds of successful outcomes and career path you desire. Certainly, there is passing resemblance between networking and Networlding - both revolve around the concept of forming relationships. But the resemblance ends once you understand the traits of Networlding.

Let's begin the conversation by highlighting two fundamental differences between "networking" and "Networlding":
1.   Networking is **transactional** – Networlding is **relational**
3.   Networking is **tactical** – Networlding is **strategic** (as well as tactical)

Insight from **Making Your Net _Work_**
Chapter 2: Working Your Net

SCRIPT: I'd like to start by getting your views about how these two approaches may differ.
  •   What comes to mind when you think of connecting with someone "transactionally"?
  •   How does that differ from when you think of connecting relationally?

FACILITATOR NOTE: Capture answers on a flip chart, and invite participants to take notes in their Participant Guidebook. Once their knowledge and understanding level have been captured, add any of the additional traits below to the conversation. Then ask participants to share a couple of stories where they have seen either networking done with a transactional or as a relational approach. Then ask they what they learned from either approach.

Networking – Transactional Approach	Networlding - Relational Approach
• Short-term	• Longer-term
• Impersonal	• Personal, friendly, helpful
• Shallow	• Deep, engaged
• Each side focuses on what they get for themselves	• Each side looks to build the relationship
• Can make one person feel used by the other	• Both people feel appreciated, respected,
• You start from what you want from the other person, such as asking outright for a referral, an introduction, a job or other favor	• You start from a mutual interest or what you can do for the other person

SCRIPT: A lot of people look at business development from a transactional side, an approach usually associated with numbers. For example, if you were in my industry of executive search – which places senior executives into the C-suites of major companies around the world – and you wanted to get two new searches a month, you might have to make thirty connections. Maybe half of those lead to meetings (so that's fifteen meetings) and, of those meetings, maybe two or three turn into searches.

Juxtapose the above scenario against another approach. My scenario may take longer in terms of development, but you'll have an opportunity for an even larger impact and the opportunity for deeper connections. This means building your network *relationally*, where you focus first on what you can do for others versus *transactionally*, where you focus, first, on what you can do for yourself

Many people take a transactional approach as they implement a very traditional form of networking. Here, your goal may be to just get a referral or, at the very least, an introduction to new connections who could lead to new business or a job opportunity. But, often, this approach actually limits your opportunities because those with whom you network end up feeling as if they've been used rather than helped.

In contrast, a relational approach is more strategic and enlightened. Here, you recognize that those you connect with are *networking* **partners**. As partners, you both have many more possibilities to exchange opportunities over and over again. Further, you'll find that that your opportunities will expand because you stayed connected, building better, deeper, more significant relationships.

Social scientists and social psychologists often reference the science of influence and persuasion with a focus on what is termed the of rule of reciprocity. This is a social rule that states that people will give you back something equal to or greater than what you give them. Robert Cialdini, best-selling author of books on influence and persuasion, emphasizes that the Rule of Reciprocity exists in all cultures. Throughout this course, we will show you how taking this rule and applying it to your networking initiatives will help you achieve success in your business or career faster and better.

FACILITATOR NOTE: Ask participants: How many people should you nurture and maintain connections with, in order to be successful? A few, dozens, hundreds or maybe thousands?

SCRIPT: The online social media boom makes it seem like you need hundreds or thousands of connections, followers and "likes" on everything that you do. However, contrary to this approach to growing your network, you can become very successful by building a small group of well-chosen relationships. In fact, this is the most effective way to achieve your goals.

FACILITATOR NOTE: Ask participants how many meaningful relationships they think a person can sustain at any time.

SCRIPT: Robin Dunbar was the first researcher to point out that none of us can sustain meaningful relationships with much more than 150 people at any one time. His discovery is referred to as Dunbar's number.[1] Building on his findings, it's much more effective to start by building ongoing exchanges with a much smaller, high-quality network.

What we've learned is that networking as most people define it today, is rarely effective. You can have twenty-five thousand names in your online database, but the most meaningful, sustainable connections, most of the time, are those in your 10-50 person circle.

FACILITATOR NOTE: Refer participants to the **Hierarchy of Networking** diagram in their Participant Guidebook.

SCRIPT: The **Hierarchy of Networking** diagram shares the various levels you can attain when you network strategically using our focus on building relationally rather than transactionally.

HIERARCHY OF
NETWORKING

Level 5 — CONNECTION HUBS

Level 4 — SPONSORSHIPS

Level 3 — MENTORING/STRATEGIC ALLIANCES/PARTNERING

Level 2 — STRATEGIC NETWORKING

Level 1 — TRADITIONAL NETWORKING

Here are explanations of each level:

Level 1: Traditional networking: This is, more often than not, haphazard and random. You're lucky if you get a few results from all those "social gatherings."

Level 2: Strategic networking: Now you're on the right path. You focus on quality connections for the longer term with a goal of helping first. From here you build sustainable relationships with networking partners with whom you regularly *exchange* opportunities.

Level 3: Mentoring, strategic alliances, partnering: You consistently grow your networking partnerships into lifelong professional friendships of mutual support. These are people who not only help you realize your goals but they are also part of *how* you reach your goals. Along the way they offer lots of wisdom along with introductions and referrals to new people and opportunities.

Level 4: Sponsorships: Here you *champion* one another into greater positions of influence. This involves promoting each other throughout the process of getting new business or career opportunities.

Level 5: Connection Hubs: Now you've hit your stride. You are creating *connection hubs*, powerful networks that yield continuous new opportunities for everyone

---

[1] Maria Konnikova, "The Limits of Friendship," *New Yorker,* October 7, 2014, http://www.newyorker.com/science/maria-konnikova/social-media-affect-math-dunbar-number-friendships

involved. These might include clubs, networking groups, and committees that you create and lead.

NOTE: When you are working all the networking levels, above, you are in the zone of both **Making Your Net *Work* and Networlding.**

LESSON 3 - WHY DO PEOPLE DISLIKE NETWORKING?

(15-20 minutes)

Insight from Making Your Net *Work*
Chapter 3: Ten Reasons Why People Dislike Networking

SCRIPT: Lesson 2 continues to set the stage for the course by highlighting some of the negative feelings people may have about networking that can hold them back from developing this critical aspect of their careers. To begin, in your Participant Guidebook, please write down 3 common negative feelings about networking that you may hold or you may have heard others express about the process of networking – dislikes, fears, challenges, etc. What are some of the hurdles?

Keeping your list in mind, let's look at ten of the most common reasons why people dislike networking. Perhaps you can relate to one or more of these.

FACILITATOR NOTE: The **Ten Reasons Why People Dislike Networking** listed below are discussed in depth in Chapter 3 in *Making Your Net Work*. The material in the book can be used to elaborate your discussion about each point. For each topic, acknowledge the concern/challenge, but also draw positive points/strategies from the discussion in the book.

As you review each "reason," ask participants to take notes on the items that are especially challenging to them personally, and to contribute any thoughts they have about that factor (e.g., Is this a feeling they share – either now or at some point in their careers? Do they have a story to tell about this type of obstacle/attempts to overcome it?).

Ten Reasons Why People Dislike Networking
1. They feel awkward
2. Not knowing who to approach
3. Not knowing what to say
4. Fearing rejection
5. Feeling pressured
6. Feeling like a pest
7. Having trouble keeping track of contacts
8. Not always feeling up to it
9. Believing that networking is a waste of time
10. Feeling dirty

DEBRIEF: Take a minute now to review your "reasons" list. Keep those in mind as we begin to explore the Networlding approach in the next lesson.

LESSON 4 - NETWORKING VS. NETWORLDING

(15-20 minutes)

FACILITATOR NOTE: Ask the participants to provide a few reasons why relational Networlding matters, and why it's far more effective than transactional networking.

Once they have shared their personal examples, continue with the following. As you work through these, ask participants to discuss and take notes on the differences between what you're describing for Networlding compared to common networking.

SCRIPT: <u>First,</u> the *Networlding Way* is a strategic method to stay connected to ever-changing resources, exchange and grow opportunities, and to strengthen and build transformational relationships.

The Networlding Way uses the science of networks and art of building your network along with the advantages of social media and today's technologies to provide the ability to make a difference in energized and expansive ways not possible by just networking. It combines high tech *and* high touch.

The Networlding 7-step process is built on a foundation of the following four values:
1. Making a difference
2. Innovation
3. Collaboration
4. Integrity

Relationships that develop from Networlding:
- are connected beyond a task
- have shifted from *me* to *WE*
- have communication that includes focused listening, articulated goals, vision and an appreciation of diversity and inclusion.

Insight from **Making Your Net *Work***
Chapter 4: Create Value for Those in Your Network

<u>Second,</u> the foundation for building a net that *works* starts with creating value for those in your network. Here, begin with the question, "How can I help?" This enables, first, a *connection*, and then a *direction* to your conversation.

It's about making a plan for your life that helps others get where they want to be. I embrace what leading motivational speaker Zig Ziglar once said, "You can get everything in life you want, if you will just help enough other people get what they want."

We're sure you've met people who come at networking purely systematically, not from the heart or with the intention to help others. If you're one of these people, I want you to know that there's a part of this that you'll be very good at—the *science* of creating networks. But to be truly successful, you have to learn the *art* that includes the emotional elements of networking and the creativity that helps you see possibilities in relationships that others who take a strictly logical approach can miss.

Networking takes tact and creativity, what I would term the *art* side. But it also takes strategy, the *science* side, to create value for both parties to continue building connection and support for one another.

I get it that many people don't understand this starting path to add value to your network. Many say, "I have to work at networking. I only do it because it makes sense to connect with colleagues and clients." I have to work at it, too. But because I'm aware that so many people have problems with it, over time I developed a process that helps me move past any issues I may have with networking to focus instead on how I can help others. This is all about starting to add value to that person by building a connection. It's about *giving first*.

There are three basic but important steps in my networking process, each with its own set of practices, each important and even essential to success:

1. Find common ground: values, and interests between you and the person I'm networking with. This step lays the groundwork for the next two steps.
2. Ask questions like, "What do you currently need?" and "How can I be helpful to you?"
3. Ask the important question, "How can I connect this person to someone valuable in my network?"

We're very aware of the time this takes. The amount of time it takes to network effectively is often why many people complain that networking isn't worth the effort. However, these people fail to see that time is their *investment* in their success and, also, in the success of their networking partners. These same people won't hesitate to work to make money to buy whatever they need to achieve success, yet they don't see how building a vibrant network can dramatically accelerate their career goals.

We've also found that our investment in building a powerful network has yielded sustainable success for me and for my networking partners. You have to *give* something to *get* something. Remember the *rule of reciprocity* that I mentioned a few minutes ago? Robert Cialdini points out that this rule holds true throughout all cultures. When you give someone something, he or she feels compelled to offer something in return. Now, we are not advocating for you to give something just in order to get something. This is where the art side comes in and, even more so, a *faith* that you will be rewarded for your giving.

Third, the Networlding Way is a new way of creating meaningful relationships.

Things in our fast-paced world are constantly changing; we need to stay closely connected through our relationships. Others are receiving a constant flow of information just like you, and with their different perspectives could offer information of value to us that may have been outside of our awareness.

In Networlding, we organize our relationships in three different circles of connection: primary, secondary, and tertiary. We'll cover those types more in depth in step 2.

To help determine what connection goes into which group, look at:
- Values you share
- Your frequency of contact
- Overlapping goals
- Availability
- Level of exchange and
- Type of exchange or opportunity

Fourth, the Networlding Way uses the Networlding Support Exchange model, which you were just briefly introduced to in the icebreaker exercise and will learn more about in step 4. This model follows the natural progression of meaningful relationships.

The Networlding Support Exchange Model

The model follows seven steps. What you just saw in the icebreaker were the first two: emotional support and informational support. As you grow a relationship, you begin to share at a deeper level and create transformational opportunities over time.

The top level is creating community, or a ripple effect from multiple exchanges. And you'll notice the entire model is surrounded by fulfillment - which is ultimately what we are looking for ourselves, and looking to help others create.

Insight from **Making Your Net *Work***
Chapter 2: Working Your Net

Fifth, what we mean by *strategic* is that we are ***awake in our networks***. As we discussed earlier, that means we consciously build our connections by:

- Making time to meet new people.
- Listening deeply and asking probing questions.
- Looking for connection points: commonalities, mutual interests, or people we have in common. Creating this shared foundation helps build relationships.
- Focusing on giving first. This usually starts with asking, "How can I help you?" This approach, along with other strategies and tactics, has brought us both successful careers and fulfilling professional and personal friendships.
- Being passionate about helping people grow in their careers and businesses by managing the nuances of building their networks.

LESSON 5 - TAKE THE MAKING YOUR NET *WORK* – NETWORLDING ASSESSMENT

(20-30 minutes)

SCRIPT: This brings us to Lesson 5. We'll begin by discovering your personal beliefs and preconceptions about networking using the Assessment questionnaire you will find in your participant guide. This assessment has been adapted from **Networlding** and **Making Your Net *Work***.

Read each of the statements in the questionnaire and note how strongly they reflect your current beliefs, expectations and actions. Then add up your scores to calculate a grand total.

There are no right or wrong answers - you won't be graded and no one will see your individual responses, so answer them honestly and don't over think it! Let's take about 10 minutes to complete.

Read each statement and rate how often you are guided by these attitudes or practice these behaviors. For example, enter a 1 in the Never column or a 5 in the Always column. Then total each column, and add the totals together for a score.

Assessment Questionnaire

	Never = 1	Seldom = 2	Some-times = 3	Often = 4	Always = 5
I believe it's important to make a difference.					
I believe anything is possible.					
I believe I am guided by strong inner beliefs, intent, or principles.					
I believe in partnering with others.					
I believe that with great networking partners I can get powerful results.					
I believe people are my most creative resource.					
I share my goals with my networking partners.					
I build and nurture relationships with my networking partners.					

	Never = 1	Seldom = 2	Some-times = 3	Often = 4	Always = 5
I limit relationships with selfish individuals and those who don't help me realize my goals.					
I respect the creative process of networking.					
I believe that good networking shortens the time to achieve my goals.					
I assume that good networking is a balanced process of giving and asking for support.					
I believe that good networking can help me achieve most of my goals.					
When networking, I ask for what I need or want.					
When networking, I work to discover the interests and needs of those with whom I network.					
When networking, I expect to discover and create new opportunities for myself and my networking partners.					
I network with people who can regularly make introductions.					
I offer emotional support, informational support, and other support to my networking partners.					
I respond quickly to the requests and needs of my networking partners.					
I measure the results of networking efforts.					
Column Totals:					

Total your score: _____

SCRIPT: When you've finished, take a minute to find your place on the Networlding continuum. There are four phases to the continuum.

FACILITATOR NOTE: Briefly touch on the four phases. These same descriptions are in the Participant Guide for them to read and absorb in detail.

Phase	Description
Novice (20-44)	You're an entry-level networker. You've probably established a baseline network of friends, family members, and co-workers. You may participate in professional or community organizations, but typically novices aren't in leadership roles. You may have started to think about values-based relationships, but haven't yet begun sharing your values, goals, and beliefs with others. Some reasons people stay in the novice category can include fear of rejection, or the belief that you don't have enough value to offer. **Despite misgivings you might have about reaching out to others, start by making your goals, values, and beliefs known.**
Networker (45-64)	You are a true networker, likely to have expanded beyond your circle of family, friends, and colleagues to include those from industry associations or community organizations. You recognize influential people and make an effort to meet them. You may even have a large directory of contacts. Despite your ability to meet and greet, you are not generating the relationship quality or opportunities you desire. The contacts you've made don't necessarily represent relationships; you may not follow up on a consistent basis, or if you do establish a surface relationship the trust and shared goals have yet to be developed. **Learn to focus your efforts on developing relationships that are based on valuable exchanges. You'll begin to experience the naturally beneficial opportunities that Networlding provides.**
Strategic Networlder (65-84)	You've moved well beyond traditional networking and entered the realm of Networlding. You most likely target and qualify those with whom you spend your time, share your intent with those in your circle, grow contacts into meaningful relationships, exchange different types of support, schedule meetings and perform regular follow up, and leverage relationships to develop opportunities for yourself and others. **You are instinctively doing the right things. The next step is to broaden your skills into a systematic approach for even greater success.**
Networlding Expert (85-100)	You're a top-level Networlder. You most likely have circles with broad access to people with varied interests and skills, exchange support on all levels, acquire whatever resources you lack through others, interact with influential individuals, establish mutually beneficial opportunities, and form personal strategic alliances. **Refresh, refine, and further extend your Networlding skills and processes to achieve even greater fulfillment.**

DEBRIEF: Ask if anyone is willing to share where they are on the continuum. Ask them to circle any of the questions or statements that really stood out to them as traits they would like to specifically work on.

SCRIPT: So we've learned where we are on the continuum, and remember that Networlding is a set a steps and skills that we practice over time. No matter where you currently are on the continuum, the skills we'll learn here will help us improve or refine what we're currently doing.

There are some fill-in-the-blanks in your participant guide to follow along.

FACILITATOR NOTE: Fill-in-the blanks are underlined in the bullets below.
1. Our goals are to improve on the skills, behaviors, and mind-set that Networlding represents.
2. Focus on continuous improvement, NOT on achieving an expert status.

SCRIPT: Let's look at how we can increase our Networlding Expertise (IQ).
There are 5 key actions:

1. **Visualize your Networlding.** This is about shifting your frame of reference from a flat, static series of contacts to an evolving, multi-tiered group of connections. Picture yourself in the center of a living organism. The cells surrounding you represent your connections - all people you like and trust. Each cell provides a unique and valuable function. As the organism grows, it changes form, learns new things, and gains experience. Cells are added and replaced to keep the organism functioning as a whole. Your Networld is something that evolves and changes over time but is always functioning.

2. **Establish connections with bridgers.** Bridgers are those individuals who bring together people from different groups to develop new opportunities. Bridgers can be just about anyone - they're the ones who seem to know everyone, have a knack for anticipating who will work well together, and love to make introductions. Your Networld must have bridgers - they're the link between you and others who can become important Networlding partners.

3. **Create inner and outer circles.** Every well-functioning Networld has an inner circle and a series of outer circles. This helps you to organize your relationships and focus your energy on the right people at the right time. Your primary circle is critical.

   Within this circle are people who most closely align with your values and goals. Here you want to make a point of having frequent contact and support exchanges. This circle holds anywhere from 3-10 influential people who have an interest in not just giving or just taking, but rather, *exchanging* **all kinds of opportunities.**

   Those within your outer circles can also become great sources of information, wisdom, leads and referrals, The best way to keep your opportunities flowing here is to weekly tap into online tools, especially LinkedIn, to discover new potential Networlding partners.

4. **Identify and include influencers.** People who are influencers use their knowledge, skills, experience, reputation, and resources to make things happen. They aren't always in positions of what we consider to be traditional power. We've probably experienced someone who is considered powerful to use negative tactics, such as intimidation, to influence an outcome. True influencers affect the opinions and behaviors of others through positive means.

5. **Maximize your connectivity.** Use multiple methods, both online and offline, to create and sustain relationships. In today's world of social networking, it would create a big hole in your Networlding strategy to not use all of the tools available to you. Many connections made initially online evolve into deeper personal relationships. It's important to strike a balance with all your connection methods.

CLOSING DISCUSSION: Ask for any additional questions, comments, or takeaways that the class has uncovered before moving on to Step 1. You may also summarize the main points.

SCRIPT: The Assessment Questionnaire has provided you with a general idea of your current level of Networlding expertise and helped you identify the specific gaps you have in your current networking efforts. As a final note, it can also be a valuable tool to retake periodically to see how (or if) your approaches to networking are evolving.

STEP 1 - ESTABLISH A VALUES-RICH FOUNDATION

The first step in Networlding is creating a values-rich foundation. This step is about becoming consciously aware of our values and then creating goals and actions that reflect those values.

For this segment, you may want a flip chart or whiteboard. Participants have a corresponding guide to follow along. Take time to familiarize yourself with the participant guide.

AGENDA

Customize the agenda timing as needed.

TIME	ACTION	OBJECTIVE
60 minutes	**Lesson 1**: Creating Your Foundation	Establish values, strengths, goals, and actions
	Exercise 1: Value Priorities	
	Exercise 2: Identify Your Strengths, Goals, & Actions	
20-30 minutes	**Lesson 2**: Networlding Beliefs	Identify the common beliefs Networlders share, and how to look for them

OBJECTIVES

The objectives for Step 1:
- Discover the values that will become our foundation in creating Networlding relationships
- Identify beliefs common among Networlders, and how to look for them in others

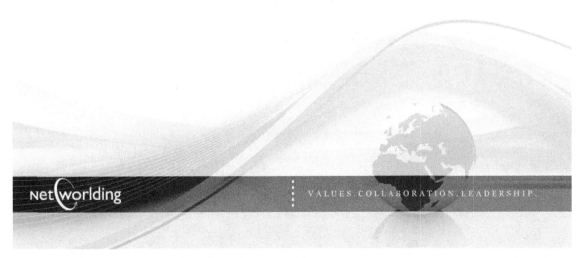

LESSON 1 - CREATING YOUR FOUNDATION

(60 minutes)

SCRIPT: Up to this point, we've compared networking to Networlding, discovered our Networlding IQ, and ways to continually improve it.

That brings us to the first step in Networlding - creating a values-rich foundation. This step is about becoming consciously aware of your values and then creating goals that reflect those values. When you stop to think about, we can often fall into the cycle of working with people or on projects that don't align with our values or goals.

Think of your values-rich foundation like a house. There are some key steps to building a house, right? Here's a summary of the steps:
1. Identify your value priorities.
2. Identify your strengths.
3. Identify your goals.
4. Create action steps that are aligned with your goals and priorities.

First, let's identify our value priorities. Your values have been established over time, but sometimes we aren't always *aware* of them. When you identify your values, you will begin to see them in those that might make great Networlding partners for you.

Values clarification is also an imperative step in the transition from doing the things you are skilled at to doing the things you are passionate about. You can be competent without being passionate about a job, project or task. **When you identify an overlap between what motivates you and where you <u>excel</u>, you've found a passion!**

If you don't define your values, you risk establishing relationships with people who operate from a valueless base. For example, have you ever done work for someone or entered into a business partnership with someone that didn't feel quite right? Like maybe you were selling out? Chances are good that person didn't operate from the same value base as you.

EXERCISE 1 - VALUE PRIORITIES

(15-20 minutes)
FACILITATOR NOTE: This exercise has 3 parts.

SCRIPT: We're going to do a short exercise to help us better uncover our values. You'll see a list of some value priorities in your guide. This isn't an exhaustive list, so feel free to add your own as you see fit. All of the values listed are important. You are identifying what drives you. For example, do not feel compelled to select "family" as a value if it is not what motivates you to action. That does not mean you don't care for your family.

Values List			
Achievement	Advancement	Adventure	Affiliation
Authority	Autonomy	Balance	Collaboration
Community	Competence	Competition	Connection
Contribution	Cooperation	Courage	Creativity
Economic Prosperity	Economic Security	Empowerment	Fame
Family	Focus	Freedom	Friendship
Fun	Giver	Happiness	Health
Helpfulness	Honoring	Inner Harmony	Integrity
Involvement	Knowing	Knowledge	Loyalty
Making a Difference	Non-judgment	Order	Personal Development
Pleasure	Power	Quality	Recognition
Responsibility	Safety	Self-Motivation	Self-Respect
Service	Spirituality	Success	Trust
Wisdom			

FACILITATOR NOTE: Your objectives are the following -
- Begin a dialogue about what the word "values" represents to participants. This will also give you an idea of where they are in their thinking process.
- Get them out of their heads and into where their cores values exist. Ideally you want the participants to experience their values.
- Inform the class that the values list is simply a list of words. We apply the meaning to the value. Values represent a state of being and what's important to us.
- Values either bring us to a certain action, or stop us from doing something. They provide internal motivation and guidance. It's the only path to authenticity and fulfillment. Sometimes when we are focus on external motivators the fulfillment is short lived (think of a shopping spree, a raise, the latest gadget.)
- Participants should become active listeners. Listening is a key skill in the Networlding process.

PART 1 - DIRECTIONS FOR FACILITATOR:

1. If you have a co-facilitator, you will want to demo this with that person. If not, ask for a volunteer from the group.
2. Ask your demo partner to select 1 value of theirs.
3. Then ask the following questions, where (value) changes to the answer of the previous question.

FACILITATOR DEMO SCRIPT: When you are experiencing _(value)_ ,

1. What do you get from _(value)_ ?
2. What does having _(value)_ do for you?
3. What is important about _(value)_ ?
4. When you have _(value)_ , what is even more important than that?

SCRIPT: Now that you have seen this demo, here's what I would like you to do:

1. Create pairs or triads.
2. One of you will take the **explorer role** (being asked the questions), one of you will be **the guide** (asks the questions and only listens, no interpreting, records words used by explorer to describe).
3. If you have a third person, that role is to observe both the guide and explorer, record words that the explorer expresses, and provide support for the guide if needed.

FACILITATOR NOTE: If it's a large group, triads work well. They should break into threes, and then the facilitator sets up the explorer, guide and observer by perhaps assigning A, B, C to the sets.

SCRIPT: As you are working through this exercise keep these things in mind:

- You could end up with a different value than the one you started with.
- Ask the questions as stated with no embellishment or elaborating.
- Listen as a witness, without interpretation, repeating back exactly as shared, with full focus on what the other person is sharing.
- It does not matter in the end what the value is called, all that matters is that it is clear to the explorer

DEBRIEF: Once they had a few minutes to go through the above exercise, bring them back for a discussion with the following:

- How did you learn from your role?
- Did anyone's value change?

PART 2 - DIRECTIONS FOR FACILITATOR:

FACILITATOR NOTE: Now that they have identified what is really important, they will now explore how they actually experience their values. Part 2 is especially helpful for one on one coaching, and may not apply to a larger group. If Part 2 does not apply to your group, move to Part 3.

SCRIPT: Now that we have worked through one value, now think about when you experience the core value and what you get from it.
1. What do you feel?
2. Where do you experience it in your body (location of feeling)?
3. What do you hear?
4. What do you see?

DEBRIEF: It's important to know when you are really in sync with your values. Because when you are aware of these feelings, when you interacting with another and you are feeling that same resonance, then you have a possible Networlding partner.

PART 3 - DIRECTIONS FOR FACILITATOR:

SCRIPT: So far we have looked at one value, and then reflected on what actually happens internally when we experience that value. Now I would like to complete a list of **four value priorities.** You are welcome to use the list in your guide for examples, but don't feel obligated to use those words. The words aren't that important - it's important to make sure the words you choose for your values have meaning to you.

Once you have identified your top 4 values, look for the graphic of a house in your guide. Now, **enter your value priorities (in order if possible) in boxes 1-4.** These values represent the foundation on which your structure is built. You will see as we move through the next sections how your values, strengths, goals, and actions create the structure for which you can apply the principles and steps of Networlding.

FACILITATOR NOTE: Below is the "Creating Your Foundation" chart that participants will see in their guide.

EXERCISE 2 - IDENTIFY YOUR STRENGTHS, GOALS, AND ACTIONS

(20 minutes)

FACILITATOR NOTE: This exercise is divided into 2 parts. The first part is strengths that become the foundation of your personal brand, and the second part is your goals and the milestones for actions you will take to achieve your goals.

PART 1 - STRENGTHS AND YOUR BRAND

Insight from **Making Your Net *Work***
Chapter 7: Your Brand Story and Your Networking Brand

SCRIPT: Now let's take a look at strengths **that set the foundation of your brand**.

Like your value priorities, strengths are a key component to your Networlding house. Strengths are those traits that best help us move forward in achieving our goals. They are qualities that come from you and contribute to your uniqueness. Uniqueness is what will set you apart; it helps you to be viewed as an influencer in your area of expertise.

Strategic networking starts with building a values-based personal brand. Think about hiring decisions. People get hired for their strong brand, their capabilities and track record of success. Let's say there are ten people who might be suited for a certain position, all of whom are well-qualified. The hiring manager wants to find the person who fits the *culture and has the skill sets* of the organization. In order to do this, they have to really know each person. This *connection process* puts people in positions where they can play to their *strengths*—where they can be most successful.

So what is your personal brand? Start by taking an inventory by answering the following questions:

DIRECTIONS FOR FACILITATOR AND SCRIPT:

1. Ask the participants to reflect on the following questions listed in their guide.
   a. What makes you unique?
   b. What do you love to do?
   c. What do you do better than anyone else?
   d. What are you known for at work? For example, it might be your ability to listen well, or perhaps you are the person who plans all the outings for your team or maybe you are the connector who is constantly introducing the new people to those seasoned in your organization.
   e. What resources (your own and from others) do you have available to you?
   f. What do people that you know you well see as your strengths?
   g. How would others that you trust describe you?

2. After reflecting on those questions, ask them to list their top 3 strengths. It might be helpful to consider strengths in the context of your environment where you spend a lot of time. For example, if you are researcher and spend time with others in the same role, what make you stand out? In other words, avoid confusing a current professional or personal role as a strength, but see where your uniqueness shines.

3. **Fill those strengths into boxes 5-7.**

SCRIPT: You have a brand story as an individual, about *why* you have become who you are. This question of why you are doing what you are doing now, stems strongly from the people you met and built relationships with throughout the years.

Because of these relationships, opportunities emerged: you took job A or opportunity Z. Your unique connections created the story you now share with others when they ask, "How did you get to where you are today?" And, for better or worse, you have a story that has emerged from your connections. This is your *brand story.*

Here's an exercise you might want to try sometime. Take a sheet of paper and write at the top of it, "Why?" This is where you can start writing your networking brand story. Why are you doing what you are currently doing in your professional life? What made you choose the path you are on? How, after others helped or blocked you path to success? What is your vision for success? How could your network support your vision turning into a reality? All of these questions and your responses will help you develop your story.

Following are tips to creating your own successful brand:
- Really understand that the right connections make the difference. Find even one *right* connection for your network as soon as possible.
- Don't wait for someone else to make connections for you. Take charge.
- Don't stop until you get to the "yes." I had sixteen nos before I got a yes. Persevere.
- Stay optimistic. If you're not optimistic about your career, who will be?
- Start your plan early.
- You can always change course, but you need to have a plan.

My professional brand is different from my personal brand, but they're connected. I see combining them as a powerful networking tool. If I end my employment tomorrow, I won't have to restart my network. I've created networks around the things I'm most passionate about, not just my job or my industry. I don't have a start time or a stop time when it comes to networking. The power of my networks is that they're about helping people, not just leveraging my position or employment or title.

I'm deliberate and strategic with:
- Making time for others.
- Leading with the question, "How can I help you?"
- Having both a short- and long-term payoff mentality.
- Incorporating networking into my everyday lifestyle.
- Developing actionable next steps.

Here are some takeaways:

- Practice sharing your networking brand story or the genesis of your story with your current networking partners.
- Ask your networking partners to share their networking brand stories. As you help them create their stories, you will get more insights as to how to develop your story.
- Look at LinkedIn profiles of people with the same background as yours to see how they present themselves. As LinkedIn becomes more social with an edge around the *art* side of networking, we've seen profiles that very effectively share impactful networking brand stories.

PART 2 -GOALS AND ACTION STEPS

SCRIPT: So far you have taken a look at our value priorities and strengths - and we've done quite a bit of internal work to help us identify those pieces.

Now, let's take a look at **goals.** You can set Networlding goals now that we're aware of our most important values and strengths. Our goals represent the above-ground structure of the house.

We've all done goal-setting exercises before.

- What prevents us from achieving goals?

FACILITATOR NOTE: Allow time to answer.

SCRIPT: Many times we set goals based as to what's logical - what we think we should be doing or what we think others expect from us. Sometimes we aren't held accountable to the goal, so we don't achieve it.

When considering your goal, it might be a professional goal like meeting a quarterly objective, or a personal goal like becoming more involved in a volunteer organization.

As far as a timeframe goes, that is up to you. we would recommend looking at nothing longer than a yearly goal.

There are two stipulations for the goal:

1. It must be consistent with your values and be specific - something you can get fired up about!
2. It must be realistic to either achieve the goal or make significant progress on in the next 60-90 days. **I'd like for you to set one goal and enter that into box 8.**

FACILITATOR NOTE: Allow them several minutes to come up with a goal and enter it into their guide.

SCRIPT: We now have the foundation of our house, our values, and the above-ground structure of our house, our strengths and goals.

<u>Now we can move on to</u> **actions** - the steps we take to achieve the goals.

There are three boxes (#9-11) for you to play with actions. Let's take the opportunity to brainstorm with our tablemates. Spend the next 10 minutes sharing with one another (as you feel comfortable) your values, strengths and the goal you've set.

Help one another with some actionable ideas - sometimes it takes an outside perspective to help us with our strategies. You might also brainstorm any potential roadblocks and how to get around them.

Fill in some action step possibilities in boxes 9-11.

DEBRIEF:
1. Ask the participants if they're willing to share the "house" they've built.
2. Ask them to share any insights from the overall lesson.
3. Mention that what they have done in sharing with their tablemates has shared emotional support, informational support, and potentially some knowledge support, all steps within the Support Exchange model.
4. Ask for any closing comments or questions before moving to the next lesson.

LESSON 2 - NETWORKING BELIEFS

(20-30 minutes)

SCRIPT: When you begin networking with others in a values-based way (like the house you just built), you will naturally be led to others who are pursuing their goals based on values. Those people will also be naturally attracted to you.

Think of your Networld like a web. A web has many different points. These points represent your connections. Picture yourself in the center of the web. Those points are varying degrees of distance from the center and create circles, or your Networlding circles.

And what holds the Networld web together?

FACILITATOR NOTE: Allow time to answer. **Answer is beliefs.** This graphic is also in the participant guide.

SCRIPT: What are the Networlding beliefs? You will find some blank spaces in your participant workbook to fill these in.

FACILITATOR NOTE: There are blanks in the participant guide that correspond with these 6 beliefs. As an option, you may ask them to capture their ideas on a whiteboard or flip chart prior to providing these beliefs. **Answers are underlined below in bold.**

1. **Anything is possible with the support of others.** Networlders don't go it alone, and especially in this 2.0 world. Values-based goals are rarely, if ever, achieved by one person alone. Relationships are what help achieve greatness.

2. **It's important to make a difference.** Making a difference means affecting others in a significant, meaningful way. It's not surprising that Networlders serve in a volunteer capacity for causes they are passionate about. And a side benefit to that is a diverse Networld, plus the chance to demonstrate skills and knowledge to a new group of people.

3. **You get what you ask for.** Networlders are willing to ask for what they need to achieve a goal. Not only do Networlders ask, but they are also willing to give a significant amount in return.

4. **All resources will be provided to reach your goals.** Have you ever had a goal, and the first thing you think is "How am I going to find what I need to make this happen? Where do I even start?" Networlders have an inherent belief that when they set a goal, and deeply believe in that goal, that the right resources are out there to achieve it. This doesn't mean they believe resources will magically appear; what it means is that they are willing to put forth the effort and make the necessary relationships upfront that will lead them to the resources they need.

5. **Life is filled with abundance and opportunities.** Some traditional networkers operate on the assumption that there are certain places and situations reserved for making connections and doing business. In contrast, Networlders operate from an abundance mindset - and that opens them up to all sorts of opportunities. They recognize that relationships are formed in many places - as a result they often form more abundant connections.

6. **There must be mutual rewards for partners.** In a Networld, mutual rewards always outweigh individual rewards. Networlders are always thinking about how they can help the others in their Networld. Networlding partners are highly respectful of one another and believe that when everyone wins the partnership is strengthened.

CLOSING DISCUSSION: Ask the class to share any examples of where they have seen these beliefs in action.
- Examples could include business, volunteer, or community initiatives where they have seen or benefited from these values. They might also share an example of where these beliefs weren't in place and the outcomes.
- Be prepared to have an example of your own to share.
- You may summarize the main points of this step before moving to step 2.

NOTES

Add any notes here.

STEP 2 - MAKE CONNECTIONS FOR YOUR PRIMARY CIRCLE

The second step in Networlding is making connections for your primary circle. This step builds upon the values identified in step 1. In step 2, participants will begin to create a list of potential Networld connections and then winnow it down to its essence based on emotional, business, cognitive, and value factors.

For this segment, you may want a flip chart or whiteboard. Participants have a corresponding guide to follow along. Take time to familiarize yourself with the participant guide.

AGENDA

Customize the agenda timing as needed.

TIME	ACTION	OBJECTIVE
5 minutes	Introduce Step 2	Communicate objectives
10 minutes	Review of Introduction and Step 1	Reinforce concepts from previous steps
10-15 minutes	**Lesson 1**: Contacts vs. Connections	Reinforce networking vs. Networlding; shift perspective from contacts to connections
30-40 minutes	**Lesson 2**: Creating Your Primary Circle	Create list for primary circle

OBJECTIVES

The objectives for step 2:
- A review of what was covered in the introduction and step 1
- Differentiate between a contact and connection
- Identify the qualities we want in a Networlding partner
- Create your primary circle

INTRODUCTION AND REVIEW

(15 minutes)

SCRIPT: The second step in Networlding is making connections for your primary circle. This step builds upon the values identified in step 1. In step 2, participants will begin to create a list of potential Networld connections and then winnow it down to its essence based on emotional, business, cognitive, and value factors.

In this lesson, we will:
- Review of what was covered in the introduction and step 1.
- Differentiate between a contact and connection.
- Identify the qualities we want in a Networlding partner.
- Create your primary circle.

FACILITATOR NOTE: If you are moving directly from step 1 to step 2 (for example, in a day-long setting or bootcamp), you may opt to skip this review. If there is a time lapse between steps 1 and 2 (for example, in a weekly setting), this review will help re-focus the participants.

REVIEW

DIRECTIONS FOR FACILITATOR: Use this time to create a group conversation by asking any of the questions below.

Below is a sampling of questions; customize this review to fit your needs. Questions address material covered in the introduction or Step 1.
- What are 3 traits of a networker?
- What are 3 traits of a Networlder?
- What are the 4 phases of the Networlding continuum?
- What should our goals be when improving our Networlding IQ?
- What are 3 key actions we can take to improve our Networld IQ?
- What is step 1 in creating your Networld?
- In step 1, what are the key steps to building your house?
- What two things do you need to identify to find your passion?
- What are your Networlding values?
- What are the two stipulations for setting a goal?
- What holds your Networld web together?
- What are 3 Networlding beliefs?

LESSON 1 - CONTACTS VS. CONNECTIONS

(10-15 minutes)

SCRIPT: Identifying our values is the first step to establishing the deeper connections that Networlding requires. But relationships won't magically appear because we've identified what we value - from there, we have to identify compatible people with whom we can proactively create values-based relationships.

Let's begin by talking about the difference between a contact and connection.

FACILITATOR NOTE: Ask the class for their perspective on the differences, and then describe how these parallel networking vs. Networlding. (Some examples have been filled in below). Also ask the class to describe a personal experience or story of a contact versus connection. You should be prepared to share a story as well if needed.

Contact	Connection
May be temporary for a specific opportunity	Lasts beyond one opportunity
May not share the same values	Most likely shares the same values
Is probably part of an outlying circle	Probably part of your primary circle
Lower degree of trust	Higher degree of trust
Someone you might run into periodically	Someone you make a concerted effort to remain in contact with

DEBRIEF: There are few key points to remember when looking at contacts versus connections.
- Networlders spend more time building a relatively small number of strong relationships that will ultimately produce better opportunities and meaningful results.
- Discernment is key. Networlders form thoughtful relationships based on what will be exchanged. Will support be exchanged? Can you see that other person valuing the support exchange model? Is this person open to different relationship possibilities?

LESSON 2 - CREATING YOUR PRIMARY CIRCLE

(30-40 minutes)

SCRIPT: There are 4 basic steps to creating a values-based primary circle. You can follow along in your participant guide.
  1. Identify your current contacts.
  2. Identify the qualities you want in a Networlding partner.
  3. Analyze and assess.
  4. Refine your top 5.

1. Identify your current contacts.

SCRIPT: The first step is to **identify your current contacts.** Our first instinct is sometimes to think only of business contacts, but open your mind to the possibilities of both professional and personal contacts. This holistic view gives you an exponentially greater pool of potential Networlders.

Using the baseline categories in your participant guide, take a few minutes to start listing out some contacts. We won't take time for an exhaustive list, but it should get you off to a good start so you can continue on your own.

You probably have a decently-sized list right now, even with the short amount of time we've spent on it. So how do we narrow that down?

2. Identify the qualities you want in a Networlding partner.

SCRIPT: We do that in the second step, which is to **identify the qualities you want in a Networlder**. Begin by looking back at the house you created in step 1.
  • Look again at your values, and the goal you've set for yourself. You might begin your list in the context of that goal.
  • Now think about people with whom you've had successful ventures, both professional and personal. This could be someone you partnered with on a client project, or your workout buddy that helped you train for the race you completed. Open your mind to the possibilities here.

So now, back in your guide follow these steps.
  1. Take the next few minutes to begin a list of no more than **10 people** with whom you've achieved that kind of success together or someone who supported you in accomplishing something.
  2. Next to each person's name, **list the qualities you value most about that person.** Think about what made you add that person to your list.
  3. Reflect on all of those qualities you've listed. **Select one** that stands out to you as the one you most admire.
  4. Now **select two additional qualities** from that list. (There will now be a total of 3 qualities.)
  5. Which of these qualities mesh with your own? For example, if the top quality you admire is visionary thinking, and you are strong with logistics, those two qualities may mesh to make the vision happen.

DEBRIEF: Ask for some volunteers in the class to describe their lists:
- Type of people on the list (friends, family, professional)
- Top quality they value in their list
- How their top choices mesh with their own qualities

SCRIPT: So how do you recognize a good Networlder when you meet one? In your guide, there is space for you to fill in these blanks.

FACILITATOR NOTE: Before filling in the blanks for them, you might ask the class what they think makes a good Networlder and see what they already know. You might also ask them to describe these traits first before providing the detailed explanations below. Answers for blanks are in bold below.

A good Networlder is:
1. **Supportive.** Networlders support your success; they listen and encourage.
2. **A continuous communicator.** A Networlder keeps in regular contact with his/her circle, whether or not there's an opportunity out there.
3. **Reliable and responsible.** Networlders deliver on their promises and take their responsibilities seriously.
4. **Influential.** Influence isn't necessarily based on wealth or prestige. In a Networld it's usually experience and expertise. Networlders are usually well-respected and are willing to use their influence on behalf of their partners.
5. **Knowledgeable.** Networlders have rich and varied experiences. Knowledge exchange between Networlders goes beyond information exchange - they share their real-world experiences, lessons learned, and wisdom.
6. **An active listener.** In today's multi-tasking world, many people aren't truly listening because there is so much competing for our attention and energy. But Networlders are attentive, and they try to understand where the other person is coming from and offer feedback that reflects this understanding.
7. **Empathic.** Empathy goes hand-in-hand with active listening. It's the ability to put yourself in another person's shoes and try to really understand what that person might be going through. Networlders know that the person comes before the opportunity, and never to take advantage of another.
8. **Appreciative.** This one is often overlooked, because in today's world people don't show enough appreciation for others. A Networlder truly appreciates the others around him or her and regularly expresses gratitude. It might be a hand-written thank you note or an email. Small acts of appreciation build up a wealth of good will that goes a long way. Do you know someone that you would do anything for? Probably because they show appreciation for what you do for them.
9. **Connection-conscious.** Do you know someone who has a knack for seeing and making connections? They recognize when two people should be introduced and act on it. This Networlder might connect two people with similar personal interests, or bring people together to achieve a specific goal.

3. Analyze and assess.

SCRIPT: So far we have talked about identifying your contacts and the qualities you value in your list of ten. We've also talked about the top qualities of Networlders.

Next, you'll want to <u>analyze and assess</u> to determine three key things about your primary circle. Is the person:
1. An exchanger? Exchangers:
   o Demonstrate a concern for your issues and needs
   o Attempt to make sure there's an equal exchange of information and leads
   o Make an effort to stay in touch with you.
   o Provide assistance without ever talking about how much they're doing for you or keeping score.
2. Someone with whom you can establish an emotional connection?
3. Someone you will enjoy working with?

4. Refine to your top 5.

SCRIPT: Lastly, you'll want to **refine your list to the top 5, your primary circle.** We're going to spend the next 10 minutes refining our lists. Even if you don't finish here, you should have a good start to finish on your own.

In your guide you'll see a space for your connections. Next to each connection jot down the status of your relationship, and the next action step you will take with that person.

You will also see a few helpful suggestions to keep in mind when creating your list.

FACILITATOR NOTE: Suggestions are from page 69 in the hardcover book and are listed in the participant guide. The graphic on the following page is in the participant guide; point that out to the class.

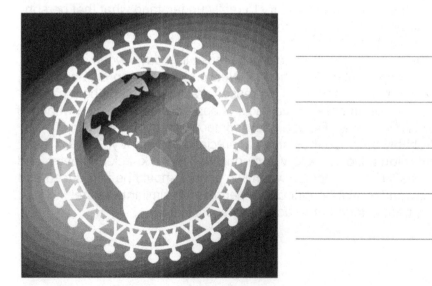

DEBRIEF: Ask for volunteers to share insights about their primary circle, with questions such as:

- How many connections are in your Primary circle?
- What challenges did you have in creating your circle?
- Do you notice any patterns about the connections in your circle?
- How many influencers are in your circle?
- What actions can you see yourself taking right away to make this circle as effective as possible?

CLOSING DISCUSSION: You may ask for further questions, comments, or takeaways from the class. You may also summarize the key points before moving to step 3.

NOTES

Add any notes here.

STEP 3 - EXPAND YOUR CIRCLES

The third step in Networlding is expanding your connections for your primary circle. While the primary circle provides you with your main center of influence, you will also need secondary and tertiary circles to build out networks.

For this segment, you may want a flip chart or whiteboard. Participants have a corresponding guide to follow along. Take time to familiarize yourself with the participant guide.

AGENDA

Customize the agenda timing as needed.

TIME	ACTION	OBJECTIVE
5 minutes	Introduce Step 3	Communicate objectives
15 minutes	Review	Review to reinforce concepts from previous steps; forge new connections in group setting
30 minutes	**Lesson 1**: The Value of Influencers	Understand qualities of influencers and how to reach them
15 minutes	**Lesson 2**: Secondary and Tertiary Circles	Expand beyond primary circles
10 minutes	**Exercise 1:** Creating Secondary and Tertiary circles	Expand beyond primary circles

OBJECTIVES

The objectives for step 3:
- A review of what has been covered so far in previous steps
- We'll learn about influencers: who they are, why they are important to your Networld, and how to reach them
- Creating secondary and tertiary circles

EXPAND YOUR CIRCLES - INTRODUCTION AND REVIEW

(15-20 MINUTES)

SCRIPT: Welcome to Networlding. Step 3: Expanding your circles. In step 2 you created your primary circle. Think of your primary circle as your first circle of influence. But you will also have secondary and tertiary circles of influence – that while less important than your primary one, they are still significant.

In this lesson, we will:
- Review of what has been covered so far in previous steps
- Uncover influencers: who they are, why they are important to your Networld, and how to reach them
- Create secondary and tertiary circles

This opening activity provides a review of the concepts we've learned and applied so far.

REVIEW

FACILITATOR NOTE: This activity is best suited for the group if they have had time away (for example, in a weekly workshop format) to absorb and apply the lessons in their life. However, it can still apply even if you are moving between steps more quickly as part of a 1- or 2-day workshop (the answers just may not be as in-depth).

DIRECTIONS FOR FACILITATOR: At group tables, ask people to pair up. There may be groups of 3 for odd numbers. As an extra step, you may even ask people to select a new table to sit at so they are able to expand their connections (Networlding in action!).

SCRIPT: As a pair or group you will ask these questions of one another. They are also in your participant guide. Use active listening and take notes in the participant guide, because you will be asked to share the information your partner gave you.
1. What is your top Networlding value and why? (From Step 1)
2. Which Networlding qualities do you most value in your connections and why? (From Step 2)
3. How has your work here so far helped you move toward the goal you set out to do? (Intro - house analogy)

The Power of 10

DEBRIEF: Ask several pairs to share their partner's story. This demonstrates active listening, plus both emotional and information exchange. You most likely won't have time for everyone.

Also ask others (ideally those who didn't volunteer) to share any other stories or insights they have learned from the Networlding process so far.

LESSON 1 - THE VALUE OF INFLUENCERS

(30 minutes)

SCRIPT: So far we have talked about the first two steps in Networlding: establishing your values and creating your primary circle. In this step we'll have the opportunity to expand our circles.

Why do we do this? Because chances are good that out of the list you created in step 2, many people aren't good Networlding candidates for one reason or another. You may need to go outside of your connections to complete your primary circle.

But the list of potential Networlding partners is your goal, and they will also have connections to others you may not know.

We'll cover three points in this lesson:
1. The importance of influencers in our Networld.
2. The common behaviors influential Networlders exhibit.
3. How we identify and reach influencers.

Let's start by talking about the **importance of influencers (1).**

DISCUSSION: Ask the class the questions below and open it up for discussion. These are also in the participant guide for note-taking.

FACILITATOR NOTE: You may want to use a flip chart to capture answers. You may also want to have a personal story of an influencer in your life that you're ready to share.
- What does influence mean to you?
- What does power mean to you? How are influence and power different?
- How do you think influence differs between a networking perspective and a Networlding perspective?
- Where have you found influencers in unusual places or situations?

DEBRIEF/SCRIPT: There are few key points to remember when understanding the importance of influence as it relates to Networlding. You can take notes in your guide.
1. Networlding defines influence as the power to affect another person, people, or course of events.
2. Networlders may have position or wealth, but they also have *earned influence* - their power to influence comes from a particular set of skills, knowledge, or experience. They aren't necessary title holders.
3. Networlding influencers are doers, not passive observers. They always add value.
4. Influencers actively work on their Networlding partners' behalf, making valuable connections, sharing resources, and making recommendations.

SCRIPT: We'll move on next to the **common behaviors that influential Networlders typically have (2).** There is space for you to enter these in your guide.

FACILITATOR NOTE: These are fill-in-the-blank in the student guide, so be sure to articulate all six.

1. **Willingness to give.** They aren't known for being generous with their time and resources and their influence is a direct result of how much they contribute to individuals and teams. Their impact stems from their willingness to share ideas, knowledge, and information that can create opportunities.
2. **Community involvement.** This is one of the most important traits for a Networlder and an influencer. Influencers purposefully expand their horizons beyond professional connections. You'll find them in volunteer organizations, heading up committees, etc. Influencers realize they can make a difference.
3. **Awareness of others' needs and interests.** Influencers routinely think beyond their own needs. That influence stems from being proactive in anticipating and responding to others - ultimately that builds trust.
4. **Dependability.** We all know dependable (and not so dependable) people. Influencers? They're dependable - they do what they say they'll do, there are no surprises.
5. **Persistence.** People who make the most impact are those that don't give up. Persistence earns respect and influence because people know that person will stick with an issue or opportunity in good times and bad.
6. **Co-visioning.** Co-visioning involves the willingness to blend one's vision with someone else's rather than insisting on a singular vision of how things should be. In many respects, a solo visionary is a symbol of networking past.

SCRIPT: So far we have talked about our perceptions of influence and some keys to remember when understanding Networlding influencers. We've also talked about six behaviors that Networlding influencers exhibit. Are there any other questions or comments before we move on?

Now we're going to talk about how **we identify influencers and then reach them (3).** Influencers aren't always easy to identify - there are many giving, community-minded, dependable people in the world. But the truth is many of them don't make an impact.

It's important to remember that impact and influence go hand in hand. Impact comes from a few attributes, and influencers have at least one of five attributes in spades.

FACILITATOR NOTE: You may want to ask participants for what they think these five attributes are before providing them. This will help you (and them) to gauge what they already know as well as provide new information. As you go, you may want to ask for stories from participants that demonstrate these attributes, or have a story or two of your own to share. These are NOT fill-in-the-blank, but the participant guide has room for notes.

1. **Broad base of knowledge.** The broader the base of knowledge, the more influential someone can be. A broad base of knowledge means that the person has knowledge of an unusually wide range of information. Most people are experts in a very narrow field. But some have knowledge that crosses boundaries. The most key element here is that these influencers with a broad base of knowledge **do** something with that knowledge - they don't just sit on it.
   o <u>Here's how you can take action</u>: When you meet others, look for conversational signs that they could have a broad knowledge base. Be careful to discern whether they are just good conversationalists or if they really are knowledgeable - a few probing questions will work. If their answers are shallow or evasive, that's a sign they lack the body of knowledge that influencers have.
   o Can you think of anyone in your life that has this attribute?

2. **Large perspective.** Influencers are big thinkers. They see possibilities where others don't. A large perspective can take many shapes. It might be a person we think of as a big visionary, but it may also be the person who takes a very complex subject and make it understandable and meaningful for others. A big thinker may not be always on the money, but they generate fresh ideas, and they aren't afraid to express them.
   o <u>Here's how you can take action</u>: Be conscious of people who surprise you with their insights. Note how they view the world and its possibilities in a different light.
   o Who do you know that's a big thinker with a large perspective?

3. **Difference makers.** Typically we associate difference-makers with high office. But look for people who use their difference-making platforms to *help others.* They help others grow their careers, they create mutually beneficial opportunities, alliances, and collaborative partnerships. Your primary circle shouldn't have only difference makers, but it's helpful to at least one person with this attribute.
   o **Mini-activity: (FACILITATOR NOTE**: Allow about 5 minutes for this mini-activity. You might ask the class to share some of their names, and if they are stuck on how to reach them ask other participants to share ideas. You might also share a personal story of how you reached out to a difference maker.)
      1. I'd like you to take a few minutes to create a list of people you might contact who are highly visible in your community or industry. This is a brainstorming list, so jot down everyone that comes to mind without judgment.
      2. Next, place a star next to those that you think have the traits of Networlders and the behaviors of influencers.
      3. From that short list, select 2-3 that you would like to contact and list one way to accomplish that.

4. **Active in organizations.** Influencers are frequently involved in a variety of trade associations, community groups, volunteer organizations, and so on. *Involvement* is the operative word here. Many people join organizations and then never actively contribute. Influencers do, and their level of activity carries weight with people and is usually shown in the variety of relationships they establish.

   o Can you think of an influencer who is actively involved in an organization, and what have you learned from that person?

   o Here's how you can take action: Think of a group you would like to join that truly interests you and does things you believe are worthwhile. It can be either professional or personal. Next, determine if there is a group member that has Networlding qualities or influencer qualities. If there is it makes sense to join the group and make that person's acquaintance. However, make sure you're not joining the group solely to meet someone.

5. **Skilled communicators.** Some *people* derive their influence from their ability to communicate with others, be it public speaking, writing, internet marketing, public relations, etc. Communications is a broad term, but we know that skilled communicators can definitely effect motivated action in others.

   o Is there a skilled communicator (can be well-known or otherwise) that has personally influenced you?

   o Here's how you can take action: Determine what communication skills you lack in reaching the goal you set to achieve (back to the house). Create a list of people who possess those skills - you may need to do a bit of research here based on what you need. For example, do you want to launch a community blog but don't know where to start? You might research other blogs, looking for patterns and reputable people as potential contacts.

SCRIPT: We've discovered the five attributes of influencers, and we know that influencers have at least one - if not several. So how do find them and **then reach them (3)**?

FACILITATOR NOTE: You may want to ask participants for their input on where to find influencers. This will help you (and them) to gauge what they already know as well as provide new information. As you go, you may want to ask for stories from participants where they found an influential person, or have a story or two of your own to share.

1. **Internet.** Use keyword searches for your industry to find thought leaders. When you get to know an influencer through his or her work, you might email that person or seek them out through social media. You can send them a note supporting their ideas and begin establishing a loose relationship. Social media especially has opened the doors to connecting with people that would be otherwise difficult to reach. I'll go into that in more detail in a moment.

2. **Periodicals.** Networlders are well-read, so you'll want to search for both online and offline publications, newspapers, books, and article directories. These are great ways to find potential influencers, and many of them may have contact information within those publications.

3. **Conferences and lectures.** When you attend a conference, keynote, or lecture do you introduce yourself to that person whenever possible? If not, you're missing a great opportunity.
   o One idea is to write a question related to the talk on the back of your business card and approach the speaker after the event. Talk with the speaker, telling him or her you enjoyed the speech and that you wrote down a question you'd like to discuss for a few minutes at some point in the next several weeks. Follow up and keep any discussion to the short time your promised. This shows your respect of that person's time, and can set the stage for future exchanges.

4. **Volunteering.** Volunteering pays off in connections when it's done from the heart. When you volunteer for a group or organization that you strongly believe in, a few things will happen. One, you're likely to support that group or organization for the long-term - allowing you to create better connections. Two, when you do meet an influencer and establish a connection at a volunteer level doing something you both love, that connection will strong and meaningful to the influencer. Some of the best opportunities in business and life come from connections based on personal interests.

5. **Program committees.** When you join an industry association, make every effort to get actively involved. The group's programming committee is a very visible place to start because you'll be connecting with influencers in that industry on a regular basis. You will also be creating continual value for the group with quality programming, and have further qualified access to group members.

6. **Lists, Directories, Alumni Groups**. Your alumni directory is a great place to start because you will already have a least somewhat warm connection if you choose to research and reach out to any people you think are influencers.
   o Use your LinkedIn groups as well. If you locate someone you think might be an influencer, look to see what other groups that person is involved in - when you share a group designation in LinkedIn, you can reach out directly to that person even if you aren't a first-degree connection.

7. **Traveling.** Use airline travel to its fullest! A lot of great conversations can be struck up at 35,000 feet. Just be careful to respect their desire to be left alone.

8. **Leisure activities.** People are sometimes mistaken that you can only meet influencers in work-related situations. Be open to meeting people in your personal activities as well. As with volunteering, some of the best connections are made when personal interests are shared. Now these people may not be influencers, but they can become a great friend, which adds balance to your Networld. And you never know when that same person can connect you with someone else of great influence!

9. **Current connections.** Everyone has hidden connections, that don't become apparent until we do some exploration. There's a psychological principle known as the "horizon of observability." In Networlding it means that sometimes we have difficulty seeing beyond our current connections. If you think of relationships as links in a chain, we don't see beyond those directly linked to us - when in reality we are connected to many other links - we just don't see it because it's not a direct connection.

- o Social media sites like LinkedIn can help "break the chain" because when you have first degree connection to someone, you also get indirect access to second and third degree connections - your "horizon of possibility."
- o Sometimes what it takes is an in-depth conversation with a current connection to be granted access to their hidden connections. You must first be willing to share a significant piece of information about yourself. All of the people you know and have formed a bond with have at least one influencer among their hidden connections.

Insight from **Making Your Net *Work***
Chapter 12: Use Social Media to Create Connections that Matter

Social media enables us to stay in contact more easily, and even make contact more easily. How do you follow up after making a connection? How do you stay in touch? Social media has created an unprecedented opportunity to keep the glue together in your networks. Some people use it better than others.

What's interesting is that after all these technological advances, fundamentally, it's still all about creating connections that matter.

Facebook, LinkedIn, and Twitter are all tools to help us connect better. At the core, social media is a networking tool. But it's *not* a network. I can use social media in addition to a phone call, a meeting, or an email. It's an instantaneous way of contacting someone. I can share a photo or an article, and I can connect you with someone else. When I'm figuring out how I can be helpful, social media can be a powerful tool.

Sometimes it's uncanny how my connections can keep tabs on what I'm doing. I won't have mentioned an event or an award, but they'll have seen it online. It's also interesting now when I talk to people during our introductory thirty-minute conversations, the other person is coming to me well-prepared. They have a good overview of me and my experience from their online research. It's social proof for them, and the thirty minutes are so much richer because some preliminaries are already known.

When you start building your network, you're using a lens. The lens I lean on the most is "diversity." I'm always looking through that lens, but unfortunately it's not what other people are commonly looking for. Some people stay in their own neighborhoods and never go downtown. But there's more diversity in major cities than in the suburbs, which are more homogenous.

The same is true for people on social media, where the majority of people connect with people they already know or people who are quite similar to them. They don't extend externally. How can people extend beyond the groups of people they already know?

Seek out new connections on Facebook or LinkedIn who might be in your same industry or social circles, but who have different backgrounds and life experiences from yours.

Helping your net *work* with LinkedIn

LinkedIn is the most business-focused and powerful social media platform for finding job opportunities, attracting qualified candidates for jobs you're seeking to fill, expanding your influence, and, of course, growing your network. Those who use it halfheartedly are missing out on a potential goldmine of leads, valuable contacts, and ear-to-the-ground information about what's happening in their industry.

Like all social media platforms, you want to establish trust with others in your network. That means being aware that what you say about yourself must be true and not exaggerated. Ask current and former colleagues to recommend you for particular skills and reciprocate by doing the same for them.

FACILITATOR NOTE: Ask participants – Who here has a LinkedIn account? Does anyone have a premium subscription? Briefly discuss the premium options:

- ***Career.*** LinkedIn claims that candidates with a Premium Career account get hired an average of two times faster than others. This plan lets you direct message recruiters or job posters through InMail, see who's viewed your profile and how they found you, become a featured applicant and move to the top of recruiters' applicant lists, and even compare yourself to other candidates. You also get access to online video courses via LinkedIn Learning.
- ***Business Plus.*** With this plan you get fifteen InMail messages per month that let you contact anyone, even if you're not connected. You can see who's viewed your profile and how they found you. You'll also find business insights into a company's growth and trends, and you'll get unlimited people browsing from search results and suggested profiles, as well as access to online video courses.
- ***Sales Navigator Professional.*** If you're a salesperson, this is the plan for you. You get twenty InMail messages, and you can see who's viewed your profile and get insights into your accounts and leads such as job changes, company growth, and more. This plan also includes unlimited people browsing, and lets you build custom lead lists with advanced search filters to help you zero in on decision-makers. You'll also get lead recommendations, and you can save leads to stay up to date.

FACILITATOR NOTE: Ask participants who have a LinkedIn account – What are the most important aspects of your profile? Include in the discussion:

- Make sure your photograph is up to date, in focus, and as professional as possible. Don't add extraneous details from the background; crop in tight so your smiling face is all the viewer sees.
- Be sure your professional headline accurately describes your role. Some examples LinkedIn offers include Experienced Transportation Executive, Web Designer and Information Architect, or Visionary Entrepreneur and Investor. Keep in mind that you have only a few seconds to grab a viewer's attention, so be succinct and not too clever.
- LinkedIn will prompt you to keep adding to your profile until you reach "all-star status." You'll want to include the schools you attended, including high school, college, and any other studies. Also, be sure to add your interests and hobbies. Whether it's gourmet cooking or cigar smoking, golf or NASCAR racing, letting people know about what you like to do in your spare time will

help others with similar interests find and connect with you. The more you share about yourself, the more people will trust you.

FACILITATOR NOTE: Ask whether anyone has taken a course on how to use LinkedIn. There are numerous online courses you can take to learn how to get the most from LinkedIn, some free, and others requiring payment. What kinds of things have you learned from a course, book or your experience on LinkedIn?

Suggestions:
- **Ask to connect:** Once you tell LinkedIn where you've worked and gone to school, the site will recommend people you might want to connect with. As we've discussed throughout this course, the *quality* of your connections is much more than the *quantity*. Only connect with people you actually know, or have met, or know people you know.
- **Engage with your community:** You can also use LinkedIn to post articles and insights about your industry to people in your network. If you're the author, you can become known as an expert, and even if all you do is forward interesting links you come across, people begin to think of you as someone who is engaged and influential.
- **Take tests and certifications:** The site also offers links to particular tests and courses that you can take to enhance your skills and verify your competence. You can take a trial course free for the first month, and the topics are targeted to your particular industry and interests.
- **Stay active:** Like any social media site, your contacts will lose interest if you're not actively posting over time. They also won't like it if they send you an InMail and you don't see it or answer it for two weeks. Check in every day if possible, or every other day if that's too much.

Helping your net *work* with Facebook

Most of us remember life before Facebook. Now it seems like everyone is spending hours a day posting pictures of their children, projects, political views, and more. Facebook is so pervasive that we seldom give it much thought. That's really unfortunate, because if you share ideas and photos on Facebook without considering who will read your posts and how they might react to them, you can quickly damage your personal brand. I always like to think of how a particular post might be viewed by my mother.

FACILITATOR NOTE: Ask participants about the best things that they have learned about using Facebook for networking. Include in the discussion:
- **Think about who might be reading your page and posts:** Building the right image on Facebook takes a lot strategic planning. You have to think about what might be interesting to your network. Your Facebook network is nothing like the business focus found on LinkedIn. It includes everyone from your 80-year-old aunt to your ex-girlfriend or boyfriend, your siblings, their friends, your cousins, in-laws, people you used to or currently work with, potential clients and future employers, former teachers or classmates—you get the picture.
- **Be conscious:** With such a wide range of people seeing your posts, you have to be careful what you say and do. Like all networking you do, you want to

build trust, and strengthen your brand. Be careful about alienating others by expressing strident political or religious views. Don't mindlessly forward some bit of news or a made-up claim that comes your way unless you do a little research and make sure it's not a rumor or falsehood. Remember, everything you post can be seen by almost anyone, and will be online virtually forever.

- **Don't brag:** Many times, it seems like people post things to Facebook only to make themselves look good. Nobody likes a show-off. People prefer self-deprecating humor, unusual occurrences, lovely photos, or pithy observations over seeing your shiny new car or ostentatious house. They like seeing pictures of you with your family and friends, and can tolerate photos of your Hawaiian vacation if they aren't meant as a way to show off.

- **Look for how you can serve:** Rather than use Facebook to make yourself look better, use it to gain insight into others' lives. When you find out someone's parent just died, or their child went off to college, consider what they might need from you. Likewise, if they've moved to a new city, reach out to them and ask them what they like or dislike about it. Did someone get laid off? Send a message letting them know you're thinking about them, and tell them you'll keep your eye out for opportunities. Does this way of networking sound familiar? It should; all through this book we've been talking about looking first for ways you can give *to* your connections rather than what you can get *from* them.

- **Discover what your connections care about:** If you're meeting a new prospect for lunch, see if you can find out more about them by studying their Facebook page. You'll discover if they have a family, what kinds of challenges they face in their daily life, maybe where they went to school or grew up, and much more. You can use this information to create a bond with someone. "I came across the photo of your daughter's ballet recital. My daughter took ballet for ten years." But be careful sharing too much of what you've found out: people don't want to feel like you've been stalking them.

- **Engage:** Don't just read other people's posts; react to them. Like, comment on, or share posts that speak to you. Try not to get into arguments when you disagree; keep things civil. Remember, when you like or share someone else's post, you're tacitly agreeing with it, and that might have implications for some of your online friends.

- **Join groups:** Groups are one of the most powerful ways you can engage a network on Facebook. There are dozens of different categories, including Local, Friends, Games, Buy and Sell, Funny, Identity & Relationships, Spiritual & Inspirational, Food, Sports, Cars & Motorcycles, Health & Fitness, News & Politics, Arts & Culture, Animals & Pets, Home & Garden, Support & Comfort, Style, Parenting, Travel & Places, Science & Tech, Professional Networking, Outdoor Activities, Neighborhood & Community, Photography, Business, School & Education, Hobby & Leisure, and Trending.With all those categories, you should be able to find a group or two that interests you. But it's more powerful for building your network if you're able to meet your new Facebook friends face-to-face and in the flesh. That's where the category "Local" comes in. By exploring the groups in your community, you'll find people you can engage with in person—always more powerful than a simple online connection.

Helping your net *work* with Twitter

SCRIPT: Twitter is the real-time social media platform. Think of it as a starting point for building a network.

- **Decide what you want to talk about:** If you're intending to use Twitter to build your network, you need a focus. If you talk about everything that pops into your head, people might not want to follow you. On the other hand, if you stick to one or two subjects, your followers will start to see you as a source of inside information on those topics.
- **Create a strong profile:** Just like LinkedIn, your profile page is important on Twitter. It gives people an understanding of who you are and what you're about with just a quick glance. Be sure it's up-to-date and compelling.
- **Follow people you want to get to know:** If there's someone you'd like to get to know, follow them and retweet their tweets. Use their Twitter handles (@marksmith) to send messages directly to them.
- **Use it to go local:** Twitter is a great way to arrange local events. #Chicago or #Miami in a tweet can help assemble a small group to meet for drinks to discuss a neighborhood issue, or a large crowd to welcome home a local hero. It's a good way to promote local events and happenings too.

Helping your net *work* with emails and texts

OK, maybe email and text messaging aren't exactly social media, but they can be valuable tools when it comes to building and maintaining your network. Send a text to a connection on a day you know they might be facing a difficult situation. It lets them know you're thinking about them and wishing them well. If you take an interesting photo, send it to one or more of your connections and ask them what they think. It's more personal to receive a photo that was sent specifically to you on your mobile phone than to come across it in a Facebook post.

A weekly or monthly email newsletter sent to a select group of your network connections can keep you top of mind. Just be sure it contains valuable information that people can use and will welcome reading.

As we said at the beginning of this chapter, social media can be a very powerful tool for building your network. But don't come to depend on it totally, because it doesn't replace the day-to-day value of personal networking and the human touch.

A few final tips:
- **Allow serendipities to happen.** People may come into your life for a reason, a season, or a lifetime, but you don't strategically say, "I'm going to go out and look for this person."
- **Look at your career in three-year increments.** That enables you to stay focused. You don't want to stay too comfortable. Decide whether you want to stay on for another three years or move on.
- **Throw yourself a challenge**. Say you're good at marketing and sales. Explore building your technology skills.

- **Get visible.** Sit on a panel or volunteer for an in-house project that's not part of your daily workload, or join a nonprofit.

Initially, you only need one networking partner in your primary circle. In an extensive study Melissa and her team conducted by interviewing two hundred executives, they discovered that the majority of people connect with only five-to-ten networking partners monthly. This means that even one person with whom you share similar or complementary values and who is ready, willing and able to become a networking partner, can create a whole new world of opportunities for you and you for them.

Again, don't think about quantity, but quality. Be selective.

LESSON 2 - SECONDARY AND TERTIARY CIRCLES

(15 minutes)

SCRIPT: We've spent a significant amount of time here discussing influencers because they can play such an important role in our Networld. We're going to combine what we've learned in this step, along with step 2 where we created our primary circle.

After we finish here, you will hopefully have a broader vision of your Networlding possibilities by expanding your circles. We'll first discuss secondary and tertiary circles, and then you will get some time to work in your guide actually creating them (or at the least the beginnings of them).

FACILITATOR NOTE: The points to follow are all listed in the participant guide so participants can follow along and take notes.

SCRIPT: Back in step 2, we started the process of creating our primary circle. In your **primary circle**:
1. You have no more than 5 people.
2. You have partners whose values are compatible with yours.
3. Circle members who manifest the behaviors and attributes of a Networlder.
4. Your partners have some ability to influence. Otherwise they are candidates better suited for your secondary circle.
5. Your main task is to develop and deepen relationships with this group.
6. Your partners are people who you interact with on a regular basis and feel closeness to - more so than those in your secondary circles.

Now expanding to your **secondary circle**, these people:
1. Have fewer values in common with you than people in your primary group.
2. Possess goals that aren't completely aligned with your goals.
3. Have areas of interests that don't match up perfectly with your own.
4. Don't possess as many traits and behaviors of Networlders as those in your primary group.
5. Lack the time or interest to meet regularly or work together on many opportunities.
   o This point is very important, because it will help you with people "sitting on the fence" between your primary and secondary circles.
   o Even if you have commonalities with someone that will make them a great primary circle member, if they lack the time or interest - you're ultimately wasting your time.

Additional points to remember with your secondary circle:

1. Add names to this group that you may have originally considered for your primary circle, but then omitted.
2. This group doesn't have to be limited to 10, so there's more margin for error.
3. Your secondary circle is a prime place to fill in any gaps in your primary circle. Add diversity that you may be missing in your primary circle to this group. This could mean skills, age, sex, ethnicity, etc.
4. It's possible that those who you initially thought would be ideal Networlders for your primary circle may no longer be a good fit for any number of reasons. An incident might make your doubt their values, or they may become involved in other interests. These individuals may be better suited to your secondary circle.

Moving to your **tertiary circle,** this group:

1. Is wide, shallow, and full of weak contacts.
2. Is often composed of exchanges involving basic information such as job openings, data, statistics, etc.
3. Usually consists of people who don't want anything beyond an information relationship (at least at this time). They may be extremely busy and don't have time devote to a relationship with you, or they may lack the experience and maturity necessary for a mutually beneficial partnership.
4. In a sense, are classic networkers. They may develop someday into Networlding relationships, but for now they are best suited to a tertiary relationship.

EXERCISE 1 - CREATING YOUR SECONDARY AND TERTIARY CIRCLES

(10-15 minutes)

SCRIPT: In this exercise, you will have an opportunity to begin creating your secondary and tertiary circles. In your participant guide you will see:
- A flow chart to help you form your circles
- A visual to help to form your three circles (transfer your primary circle connections from step 2)

FACILITATOR NOTE: Allow the group about 10 minutes to work on this. It won't be enough time to complete the activity, but will give them a start in completing it on their own. If you have allotted sufficient time for the group to complete, tailor this timing to your situation.

The full activity as shown in the participant's guide is on the following page for you to follow along. Close this activity with the debrief questions.

DEBRIEF: Ask the class to share their experience in creating their secondary and tertiary circles. You may use the following questions to guide the discussion:
- What did you notice about your existing network?
- Where are you currently spending most of your relationship-building time?
- How might your results change if you follow the 80/20 rule of Networlding (shown in the circle graphic)?
- What role do you think social media and other relationship-building tools will play in your circles?

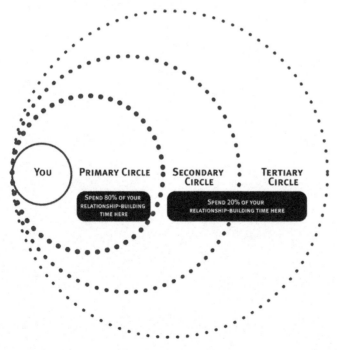

CLOSING DISCUSSION: Ask for any additional questions, comments, or takeaways that the class has uncovered before moving on to step 4. You may also summarize the main points.

Use the Networlding Circles Flowchart to help you decide your primary, secondary, and tertiary circles. Notice that it all begins with value priorities from step 1.

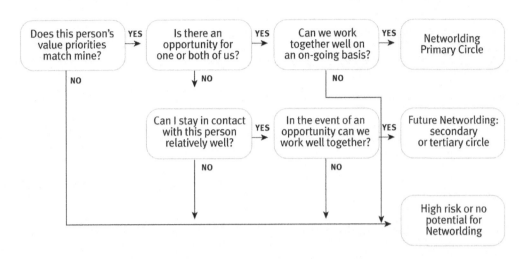

FORMING NETWORLDING CIRCLES FLOWCHART

1. Your main task is to develop and deepen relationships with people you've assigned to your primary circle. Take the following steps:
    o   Initiate contact with at least 3 people you consider prime candidates for your primary circle and who've determined to be influencers.
    o   If the response is positive, schedule a meeting or lunch.
    o   If the meeting goes well, schedule additional meetings to exchange ideas, information, feelings, and opportunities.
    o   Tap into their hidden connections.
    o   Continuously assess these 3 relationships to determine if they meet the criteria established for both Networlders and influencers.
    o   Repeat these steps whenever possible to add to your primary circle and to replace any individual who no longer belongs to that circle.

2. Your next task is to create a list of people you've designated for your secondary and tertiary circles.
    o   Stay aware of what the people in those circles are doing.
    o   Occasionally communicate with them with an eye toward determining if they're ready and willing to move into your primary circle.
    o   With your tertiary circle, keep the relationship on an informational basis.

Enter names for your primary, secondary, and tertiary circles. You may already have some connections for your primary circle from step 2. Take time to refine those primary connections based on what you've learned about influencers.

Expect this list to be dynamic, changing over time. This exercise won't result in an exhaustive list, but will help shift your perspective to thinking in terms of Networlding circles and where you invest your relationship-building time.

Primary Circle	Secondary Circle	Tertiary Circle

STEP 4 - INITIATE EXCHANGING RELATIONSHIPS

The fourth step in Networlding is about initiating exchanging relationships. The objective of every aspiring Networlder should be to establish relationships with mutual exchange as the foundation.

For this segment, you may want a flip chart or whiteboard. Participants have a corresponding guide to follow along. Take time to familiarize yourself with the participant guide.

AGENDA

Customize the agenda timing as needed.

TIME	ACTION	OBJECTIVE
5 minutes	Introduction	Communicate overall objectives
10 minutes	Review: The Domino Effect	Reinforce previous concepts; forge new connections in group setting
15-20 minutes	**Lesson 1**: Support Exchange Model	Gain more familiarity with the support exchange model
15-20 minutes	**Lesson 2**: Ingredients of an Effective Exchange	Create effective exchanges and meaningful relationships
5 minutes	**Supplement:** Questions and Expressions of Support	Supplemental questions to help with structured support conversations

OBJECTIVES

The objectives for Step 4:
- Reinforce the concepts covered so far in previous steps
- Explore the Support Exchange Model.
- Identify the ingredients of an effective exchange
- Uncover strategies for establishing meaningful contact

Net worlding   VALUES. COLLABORATION. LEADERSHIP.

REVIEW - THE DOMINO EFFECT

(10 minutes)

Insight from **Making Your Net *Work***
Chapter 5: Strategic Networking

SCRIPT: Challenges arise when you meet people who only want to meet those who can do something *for them*. This leads to an imbalance where more people are trying to help *themselves* versus helping others.

Most people feel they have more *takers* than *givers*—more people who want to take but not give to others when it came to networking. It's hard to believe that people knowingly make this their strategy for networking. The outcome over time, would only result in your network not working, as people pretty soon get wise to giving but never getting anything in return. By this we mean even receiving a thank you for what they have received.

Taking, of course, is the wrong way to approach networking. Your focus should be on making connections that are mutually beneficial. But what does that strategic process look like? How does it feel? Think about building a network with intention. Be strategic and deliberate when engaging with your networking partners by considering how to *exchange* opportunities—not just today but for the long term. One of the best questions you can ask to start this process is, "How can we create opportunities for both of us?"

Let's do an activity to review the Networlding terminology and concepts we've learned and applied so far. This will help further reinforce the importance of Networlding over networking and continue to shift your perspective toward value-based relationships.

FACILITATOR NOTE: This activity consists of a stack of 20-30 domino-type cards. Each card has a Networlding term at one end, and then the Networlding definition of another term at the other end. The activity is played using the rules of Dominoes, except that a player must lay a term against the correct definition or vice versa.

This activity can be run in small tables, or as a larger group. If it's run in small tables, you will need multiple sets of the domino cards. You may want to ask people to move tables for some new Networlding connections. If it's run in a large group, consider larger cards/print (for easier reading) and a central table where participants take turns matching the dominos. Samples are below:

Networlding	Horizon of Observability
The foreseeable number of people connected to those whom are connected to millions through our relationships with even just a few people.	

DIRECTIONS FOR FACILITATOR: Determine if you will run this activity at tables or as a large group. Time the activity, allowing 5-7 minutes for the table or group to complete.

DEBRIEF: Ask the group(s) how they did with the terminology. Time permitting, you may review all terminology, or any terms where there are specific questions. Point out that using the terminology will continue to shift their perspective toward value-based relationships.

LESSON 1 - NETWORLDING SUPPORT EXCHANGE MODEL

(15 minutes)

SCRIPT: So far we have covered three steps in the Networlding process: establishing your values, creating your primary circle, and expanding our circles.

So how do we keep all of our circles active and balanced? It's by creating relationships of exchange. More specifically as a Networlder, you need to take the initiative in establishing and creating an environment for the exchange.

There are two big challenges any Networlder faces in initiating relationships:
1. Exchanging various forms of support
2. Developing trust

FACILITATOR NOTE: You may want to use a flip chart to draw the exchange model pyramid while explaining the emotional, informational, knowledge, and promotional exchanges.

SCRIPT: The Networlding Support Exchange Model mirrors the hierarchical process involved in building any meaningful relationship. Just by looking at the entire pyramid, you can probably think of some relationships in your own business and life that have naturally modeled that flow.

There are 7 levels in the support exchange model. Within this step however we're going to cover four and the others will be covered more in detail in Networlding steps to follow. Follow along in your guide.

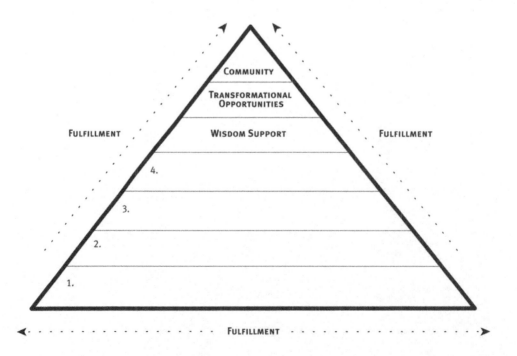

FACILITATOR NOTE: There are fill-in-the-blanks in the Participant Guide (and space for notes) for each of the 4 steps. You may also choose to review all 4 steps first before asking for examples.

Insight from **Making Your Net *Work***
Chapter 10: The Science of Making Your Net *Work*

---

1. **Emotional support.** This is the foundation of building a Networlding relationship. You may also think of it as emotional intelligence, which is the ability to understand emotions and use them to promote emotional and intellectual growth in yourself and others.

   Our feelings about others serve as the foundations for our relationships. The focus of exchanging emotional support with another is to create rapport, a relationship of mutual trust and affinity.

   People are increasingly receptive to emotional honesty, and they're looking for someone who not only says what he or she really feels, but is also an empathic listener. Emotional support builds trust and naturally allows the relationship to progress along the Support Exchange Model.

2. **Informational support.** Once at least some kind of emotional exchange has been established, people are more willing to volunteer information. But let's face it - people are overwhelmed with data and information.

   Think of all the sources you yourself have to gather information. The key here is obvious, easy-to-obtain information versus valuable not-as-well-known facts and statistics. Networlders who are especially good at information exchange are typically well-skilled in:
   - Discerning what's relevant when confronted with volumes of information.
   - Observing the world around them
   - Tuning into what type of information the other person needs.

   Once there's an initial rapport built, we then feel comfortable to share information of value.

3. **Knowledge support.** The next **natural** progression in relationship-building is knowledge support. There's a difference between knowledge and information. Information is typically pure data, while knowledge often means sharing one's conclusions, experiences, personal insights, and ideas. This level of support takes your networking to a new level as people combine the information that they acquire with their experiences. This support can provide you with both tacit (understood or implied without being stated) and implicit (suggested though not directly expressed) knowledge. Knowledge support signifies a growing level of trust. Examples of knowledge sharing may be in mastermind groups or mentoring relationships.

4. **Promotional support.** As we continue to build rapport we naturally promote the attributes of our networking partners with others in our networks. This evolves into strong word-of-mouth marketing results. This is one of the best ways to get a Networlding relationship off on the right foot. By consciously

keeping an eye out for connections between people, you put yourself in the position of offering invaluable promotion support. Think about the people within your primary circle. Can you connect them with others, or refer their business skills to other Networlders? As you promote, so too you are promoted. It's a critical exchange you want to establish quickly within the relationships.

5. **Wisdom support**: Wisdom support adds an element of selection and prioritization to the things we share with those in our network.

6. **Transformational opportunities support**: A natural result of moving up the ladder of support for our networking partners. With ongoing exchanges of support comes the evolution of opportunities that are much more robust than those that come from traditional networking.

7. **Community support**: As you and your networking partners realize transformational opportunities, it's now time to pay your blessings forward. Reach back to your networks and those communities you support or new communities you can now support.

FACILITATOR NOTE: Once you've reviewed all 4 steps, ask the class for any personal stories or examples of where they have seen the steps progress. Be prepared to share your own story as well.

(**FACILITATOR EXAMPLE:** I met someone who is now a close member of my primary circle at a training-industry association meeting. We obviously had something in common because we were both in attendance and members of the association. After the meeting ended and people were socializing, we naturally introduced ourselves to one another and established that we were both business owners.

From there we exchanged business cards and agreed to meet to learn more about one another's business. After a positive first meeting and realizing we had a lot in common both personally and professionally, we began to share business ideas and connections with one another. We both introduce the other to valuable connections, and promote one another's business in the appropriate situations.)

LESSON 2 - INGREDIENTS OF AN EFFECTIVE EXCHANGE

(15 minutes)

SCRIPT: We've spent some time talking about the first four steps in support exchange model. The remaining steps we will visit in more detail in upcoming steps.

You'll notice those steps covered the "*what*" of an exchange: emotion, information, knowledge, and promotion.

Now we'll talk about the *"how"* of an exchange.

Insight from **Making Your Net *Work***
Chapter 5: Strategic Networking.

Bob Burg, best-selling author of *The Go-Giver* and *Adversaries into Allies,* sums up what it means to have a network fueled by trust: He states, "By a network, I don't necessarily mean your customers or clients. I mean a network of people who know you, like you, and trust you. They might never buy anything from you, but they've always got you in the backs of their minds. They're people who are personally invested in seeing you succeed... They're your army of personal walking ambassadors."

What Burg is describing is what happens when you thoughtfully and strategically create networks of ongoing support. These relationships are based on building trust over time. They are also the networks where you can create what Melissa terms, *transference of trust.* This is the outcome of people either introducing you or referring you to others in their networks that you have yet to meet. The power of *transference of trust* makes for ongoing growth of the networks of all parties involved.

Starting an effective exchange is all about trust. You need to trust one another sufficiently before there's a comfort level to share valuable ideas, information, and the other forms of support. Trust allows us to:
- Move past the rough spots of failed opportunities or disagreements
- Connect beyond a single business deal
- Create an environment of openness and honesty

Let's think about a cake recipe. It usually has a certain number of ingredients, and when correctly combined and baked, creates the wonderful finished desert.
And how well that cake turns out depends on many variables: the quality of the ingredients, the right amounts of each one, the right temperature, the right time, etc. When one of those variables is off, it doesn't turn out right.

The cake is your Networlding relationship. And there are certain trust ingredients that need to be combined to create a perfect cake, or a great relationship. And the transformational opportunities that will result - is of course the icing on the cake.

Let's go back to our ingredients of trust:

FACILITATOR NOTE: Ask participants to fill in this "recipe card" as you review the ingredients of trust.

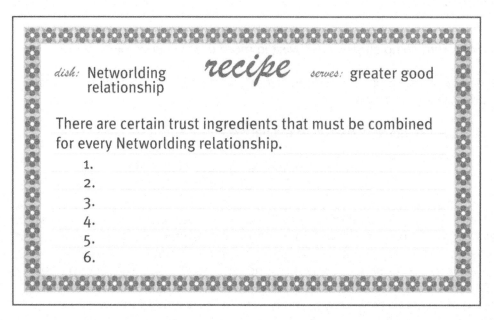

dish: Networlding relationship

recipe

serves: greater good

There are certain trust ingredients that must be combined for every Networlding relationship.

1.
2.
3.
4.
5.
6.

1. **Points of commonality.** The more common interests you share, the more potential there is for trust. Points of commonality establish a comfort level that is a pre-cursor to trust. They can include interests, skills, or hobbies. That's why often times a business relationship flows from shared personal interests. When initiating a relationship, find a way to communicate those interests that are most important to you.

> Insight from **Making Your Net *Work***
> Chapter 5: Strategic Networking.
>
> To find commonalities, it's important to know yourself well, consider the viewpoint of the person you're networking with and ask open-ended questions.
>
> People often don't probe effectively to discover what they have in common with the people they meet. Most people talk at a surface level, making small talk about things that are obvious and self-evident. They don't share interesting things about themselves that they might have in common with others, such as a love of travel, or of dogs, or art or music. As a result, they fail to connect in engaging ways; they fail to move their relationships to the next level where they can further help one another.
>
> When we break into small groups for an exercise that requires us to explore commonalities that are not self-evident, that accelerates the networking process. Share more of yourself and take more interest in other to bring that experience to your Net*work*ing.

2. **Points of credibility.** This isn't about bragging or name dropping. We all know people who do that and it's a real turn off. Instead this is about modestly and honestly communicating your contributions, strengths, and unique experiences. People tend to trust people who have achieved something unique or important - but are modest about it. Think about who you'd like to surround yourself with, those who you have credibility, or those who don't share their points of credibility?

FACILITATOR NOTE: OPTIONAL SHORT EXERCISE ON POINTS OF COMMONALITY AND CREDIBILITY (3 MINUTES). At each table, ask participants to identify among themselves points of commonality and points of credibility. This will require them to ask open-ended questions of one another, and also honestly communicate their own accomplishments and strengths.
Allow about 3 minutes for this exercise. Then debrief by asking the table to share any points of commonality or credibility that led to further relationship building at the table and what they learned from the exercise.

3. **Matching values.** Shared values make a difference in building trust. Not everyone is comfortable explicitly expressing their values, but as you get to know someone you will be able to sense what's important to them. One way to explore this area to talk with other person about what's most meaningful in your life in work. When you explain what's important and why, they might be more willing to open up and share what's meaningful to them.

4. **Tone and timing.** Do you know someone who you'd consider an "anti-Net*work*er?" Someone who's glib, slick, and superficial - says all the right things, but underneath it's not meaningful. That's why sincerity on your part in all relationships is critical, even when it's something that the other person may not want to hear. Timing is important as well. Be aware of your surroundings and of others - pay attention to when others might be open to a certain discussion, or when another time might be more appropriate.

5. **Matched communication styles.** Next time you're out and about, notice a group of people who seem very at ease with one another - you might notice they tend to use similar gestures, postures, and phrases. Likewise, when speaking or meeting with someone, pay attention to their energy level, body language, vocal pitch, speed, and words. Try to match and mirror them as much as possible in a natural way, and notice that they may seem to be more open to you. This is a simple and effective technique to make another person feel as if you're speaking the same language.

6. **Etiquette.** These points may seem obvious, but any Networlder is careful to do the following:
   o Follow-up every time and deliver on your promises.
   o Maintain eye contact during conversations. It shows your sincerity and credibility.
   o Smile! It shows you're open and eager to listen.
   o Locate people who are standing alone and introduce yourself. It shows you're caring and compassionate.
   o Give first before you ask for anything.

- o Avoid social butterfly-itis. Spend a reasonable amount of time with people you initially meet.
- o Be expressive. An interested, expressive face and body shows you're actively listening.

Insight from **Making Your Net *Work***
Chapter 5: Strategic Networking.

A final component of making your net *work* is to **build self-discipline**. Here are the steps:

- **Be in the moment.** Focus totally on the other person and what he or she indicates matters most.
- **Get engaged.** Prepare questions in advance, especially open-ended ones. See Chapter 10 for a list of questions that will create engagement on many levels.
- **Create a list of the best questions for generating conversations.** Think of the best questions you can ask to start great conversation and exchanges. For example, "If this were the best year of your life, what would you do?" Or, "What's the best question you've ever been asked?" Ask this question as often as possible of as many people as you can. Soon you'll find great, open-ended questions that unearth *possibilities* that can blossom into opportunities.
- **Keep asking questions.** When *you* do the asking you can lead the conversation toward the most successful outcome and that outcome should be about both you and your networking partners gaining value. Also, ask questions to keep both you and those with whom you are networking participating in a healthy exchange of ideas, information, and, opportunities.
- **Track what your networking partners are saying.** Focus on listening deeply to gain an understanding of what matters most to your networking partners.
- **Put the desires and any requests of those with whom you network into your mental filing cabinet.** When you take the time to take note of what matters to your networking partners and then look out for connections and opportunities for them, you set into play a significant *spirit of reciprocity* to receive the same as you give.
- **Look for connection points.** For example, if you were both from Texas, you can build on this connection. Try this even with people you already know. You will be surprised that you will very likely discover things you didn't realize you had in common. For example, Melissa was recently with a colleague she had known for years and they both just discovered they were originally from Cleveland.
- **Get to the point where you ask, "How can I help you?"** Be prepared to take some time with this step. It requires patience, as many people are not used to being asked this question. I usually have a sense of how I can help someone before I ask, but I ask anyway. Never assume.
- **Agree on your respective next steps.** Don't leave without these. Set a follow-up date for when you will reconnect and make a list of things you each will do to help one another.

As we strategically implement the science of networking, we should always keep in mind the art. This is where the human, intuitive side of things comes into play. Here are some thoughts to help you do just that:

- **Become an active listener.** Listen for understanding instead of for information. Your attention to your networking partner's needs and interests will help you create opportunities that can lead to even more and better networking exchanges.
- **Stay open to new ideas.** Appreciate the new information or different way of looking at things your network partners offer. Even if you don't agree with them, respect their opinions. Successful networking comes from being open to the different viewpoints and ideas others share.
- **Stay genuine.** Being prepared is great, but without sincerity and transparency, you have nothing. When you're genuine and sincere, you'll attract people to you who naturally want to help you. Become interested in others. Then find out what matters most to them and center your conversations around their priorities. In turn, share your priorities. Network with those who care what matters to you as much as they care about what matters to them. Again, we are recognizing the focus on the few, not the many. As Melissa points out consistently, "You are only as strong as your weakest link. Therefore, weed out those weak links in your network.

SCRIPT CONTINUES: So far we have talked about 4 of the 7 levels of exchanging support, and we've talked about trust as a key ingredient in creating those exchanges.

Now, we need to talk about specifically how you can begin to establish meaningful contact. No matter how outgoing or seasoned you may be in Networlding principles, it can be difficult to approach people.

Here are some specific tactics you can use to ease the path to initiating relationships. You can enter these in your participant guide.

FACILITATOR NOTE: You may ask participants to share any of their own tactics, or share an example of where one of these ideas worked for them. Be prepared to share an example of your own.

1. **Seek relationships in the "easiest" places first.** Look at all of the possible opportunities in front of you - events you are attending, volunteer activities, customer interactions - these are all opportunities for you to look for new relationships to build. Look at your "routine" activities in a new light.

2. **Always be prepared.** Never go into a relationship-building situation cold. Especially if it's an event where you will encounter a lot of unfamiliar faces. For example, if you are attending an event, make an effort to contact the event organizer to introduce yourself and ask a couple of open-ended questions about the organization. This builds rapport, helps you learn more about the event/organization, and will give you more confidence.

3. **Seek connections even if you don't want to.** Accept the fact that there will be times when you just won't feel like reaching out to people. But ironically enough,

these are often the times you make some of the best connections! Keep yourself in check by envisioning the incredible Networld you're constructing with these connections.

4. **Learn from rejection.** Rejection is a really common fear and holds people back from attempting to make a meaningful connection. It's not always easy to do, but try to look at rejection objectively and realize that some connections may just not happen as we want them to. It might help to write a short "anti-rejection" affirmation statement that helps you through those times. For example, "I'm a kind, honest person who sincerely wants to succeed and help others whenever possible."

5. **Create a positive image.** Remember, that you are your brand! Your appearance, attitude, and behaviors matter. It's your responsibility to project a positive image and attract others to you. Be aware of your words and actions around others. One simple way to project a positive image - smile sincerely!

6. **Build appreciation into your conversations with others.** Look for ways to sincerely show appreciation for others - it may be a compliment, a thank you note, or an acknowledgement of how they handled a particular situation. People don't get enough sincere appreciation and will remember you for it.

7. **Ask the same question twice.** This might sound counterintuitive because we think it shows we weren't listening. But in reality, it can show we're active listening to all communication, verbal and non-verbal. One example is you ask someone "How are you?" and you get a short answer, "I'm good," but you sense that's not the case. If you ask again, "How are you - really?" chances are they may open up and begin an exchange.

8. **Ask for an introduction.** Be willing to ask for an introduction from someone if you feel a real connection has been made. Be careful not to overstep your bounds, especially if you haven't yet been able to offer a support exchange with that person. But many times, people are willing to introduce you to someone in the initial stages of a Networlding relationship, because it's not a referral but simply a connection.

9. **Arrange another conversation.** Don't let your connection lose its momentum! Always follow-up on a great conversation by suggesting another meeting or conversation. Don't assume the other person will take the initiative.

Insight from **Making Your Net *Work***
Chapter 5: Strategic Networking.

---

10. **Initiate value-based relationships by telling your story.** Consider this tactic for Net*work*ing in a group. Ask the group: "Why don't we go around the table and share our stories?" Steve Pemberton, Chief Diversity Officer at Walgreens, says in his great book, *A Chance in the World*, "We don't look like our stories." You will be surprised and generate a great amount of interest and curiosity about peoples' lives.

11. **Network down as well as up.** Networking down is about being the mentor. Take one colleague of ours, Dave, a president of a large web-design and development company. He acquired a large account because he had befriended and mentored one of their salespeople several years earlier when everyone else would not give this person the time of day. But Dave realized that all people are worth the time it takes to let them know they're important and to provide them with guidance as to how to grow successfully.

12. **Treat each person you meet with uncompromising respect.** Great networkers are zealots of respect and integrity. They're like the knights in King Arthur's roundtable. They care about creating relationships of honor.

13. **Suspend judgment when you meet someone new.** We often find ourselves meeting people who, upon first glance, don't seem to have the wherewithal to exchange or just don't seem like the sharing type. However, we make it a rule to give each person the opportunity to exchange with us toward the possibility of partnership. We constantly mentor others toward becoming better partners. We see this as a way to teach the world through these people–how to be better at sharing. For instance,

14. **Be creative when thinking of people to contact.** Start with people who really like you and brainstorm with them. Get them to give you a few names of people they really like but for one reason or another you have never met.

15. **Connect the unconnected.** The research on human networks shows us that the real secret to creating a diverse, continuous and ever-growing flow of new business or career opportunities is to look for people who have yet to be connected. By linking people together, you create value for both of them.

16. **Help people feel wanted.** Recognize that most people want attention. Search for the uniqueness in others. Help them to feel significant. Do this by finding just one or two things about what they have said that you find most beneficial to you. Disclose your thoughts in a blog post or in person or mention them on Twitter.

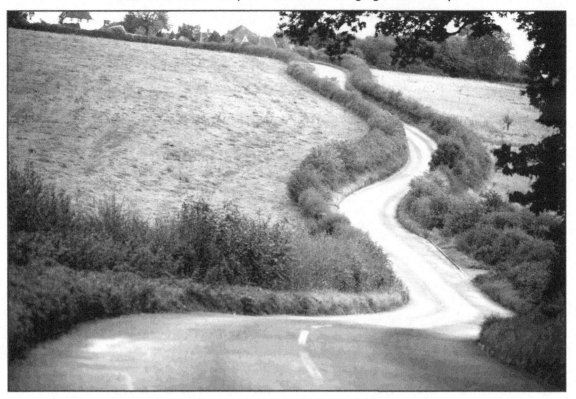

SUPPLEMENT - SUPPORT EXCHANGE MODEL QUESTIONS AND EXPRESSIONS OF SUPPORT

FACILITATOR NOTE: This section is a supplement to this step in the Networlding process, and not something that needs to be taught. Point out to the class the questions in the participant guide under this heading, for their support.

SCRIPT: An effective conversation with someone you are just meeting starts with questions that speak to the interests and needs of the person with whom you are speaking.

Finding out, first, what matters currently to someone you are talking with and second, working a conversation around what matters to them and to you, will grow a strong and lasting foundation for ongoing exchanges. There are questions and expressions for each stage of the model in your participant guide. As you practice weaving these questions and expressions into your conversations, add your own to the list!

CLOSING DISCUSSION: Ask for any additional questions, comments, or takeaways that the class has uncovered before moving on to step 5. You may also summarize the main points.

STEP 5 - GROW AND NURTURE RELATIONSHIPS

The fifth step in Networlding extends an initial exchange, with techniques to grow and nurture a relationship. The goal is to achieve even more dynamic and beneficial exchanges, moving along the Support Exchange Model.

For this segment, you may want a flip chart or whiteboard. Participants have a corresponding guide to follow along. Familiarize yourself with the participant guide.

AGENDA

Customize the agenda timing as needed.

TIME	ACTION	OBJECTIVE
5 minutes	Introduction	Communicate overall objectives
5 minutes	**Exercise 1**: Exchange Circle	Create new connections in a group setting; demonstrate aspects of the exchange model
15 minutes	**Lesson 1:** Maximizing Networlding Interactions	Realize the value of regular interactions and provide specific steps to ongoing exchanges
15-20 minutes	**Lesson 2:** Communicate on a More Meaningful Level	Practice effective exchanges and building meaningful relationships
20-30 minutes	**Exercise 2**: Meaningful Communication Role Play	Practice meaningful communication in a realistic role-play situation
N/A	**Supplement:** Networlding Exchange summary Tool	Point out that this tool is in their guides. It is a great way to help them document and capitalize on primary-circle interactions.

OBJECTIVES

- Demonstrate and reinforce steps in the Support Exchange Model (through the Exchange Circle activity)
- Maximize your Networlding interactions
- Identify ways to improve communication skills so that exchanges are more meaningful
- Practice meaningful communication in a role-play situation

Networlding

VALUES. COLLABORATION. LEADERSHIP.

EXERCISE 1 - EXCHANGE CIRCLE

(15 minutes)

SCRIPT: This activity is called the Exchange Circle. This models your Networlding circles and several steps within the exchange model. Plus we get to move around and hopefully meet some new potential Networlding partners!

FACILITATOR NOTE: For this activity, people will form a large circle. Depending on how many participants you have, decide whether to run this in one group or multiple. Ten people per group is about the max.

DIRECTIONS FOR FACILITATOR: First determine if you will run this activity in one or multiple circles. Time the activity, allowing 5-7 minutes.
1. Ask the group to assemble in a circle.
2. Within the circle, one person volunteers to come to the center.
3. The person in the center asks a question of the group that reflects something he/she enjoys doing, a place he/she has traveled, something about his/her business - the possibilities are endless. The goal is find common ground, as with a Networlding exchange. For example, "Who enjoys reading mystery novels?" or "Who is an entrepreneur?"
4. What happens next is like musical chairs. Each person in the circle (including the center person) that likes mystery novels is to move, finding a spot vacated by another mover who likes mystery novels. Let's say you have 4 movers in the outer circle, plus the center person. There will be one person left over who didn't get to a vacated spot quickly enough. That person now becomes the center person and asks a question of the group.
5. Repeat this process until each person (or as many as you have time for) has had the opportunity to be in the circle's center once.
6. Ask the class to return to their seats and proceed with the debrief.

DEBRIEF: Ask the class what they took away from this exercise. Point out that Networlding partnerships require us to:
- Be open to learning more about others
- Step outside of our comfort zones
- Be curious and ask questions to find common ground
- Begin creating and then maintaining trust
- Be proactive

LESSON 1 - MAXIMIZE NETWORLDING INTERACTIONS

(15 minutes)

SCRIPT: Let's quickly review the steps we've covered so far:
- In step 1, we created a values-based foundation from which to begin Networlding relationships
- In step 2, we created our primary circle - those 10 individuals with whom we share our closest connections and the possibilities to Networld.
- In step 3, we took that a step further to expand our circles - learning the value of influencers, and creating our secondary and tertiary circles - and expanding our horizons of observability.
- In step 4, we became more familiar with the Support Exchange Model, and discussed the first four areas within that model: emotional, informational, knowledge, and promotional support. A Networlding relationship naturally follows the support exchange model, with the big goals of creating transformational opportunities and community.

Now in Step 5, we're going to discover how we grow and nurture those relationships. It's in growing and nurturing relationships - especially with our primary circle - that will make a difference in how successful we become at Networlding.

Growing your Networld is like growing a garden - it takes time, effort, care, and consistent action, It also takes mutual trust to create results. Before we talk about Networlding content, I'd like to get your input first.

SCRIPT (CLASS DISCUSSION):
- What have you done to successfully grow and nurture business relationships?
- How do you actively build mutual trust in your relationships?

FACILITATOR NOTE: Capture answers on a whiteboard or flip chart.

Capture answers on a whiteboard or flip chart. You may want to share any stories here, or ask the class for any examples.

SCRIPT: Great input everyone. Growing and nurturing relationships can be a challenging assignment because we feel often times as though we don't have enough time to dedicate to it. Ironically, we're more connected than ever via the Internet, but inside we often feel disconnected.

Networlding aspires to create a framework where we maximize our relationship-building time. We aren't frantically searching for contacts, but focusing on growing deeper relationships with the right people, people who are potential Networlding partners.

We've started this conversation with your ideas for growing and nurturing relationships. Let's continue by looking at some other ideas.

FACILITATOR NOTE: Be prepared with a story or two to illustrate and reinforce any of these points. There is space within the participant guide for notes on these next points.

How do we maximize our connections?
1. **Schedule time for regular interactions.** Without a conscious time commitment (even if it's short) a budding relationship will fail to thrive. Ideally, set aside time on a monthly basis to share opportunities with your Networlding partnership. Find the ways to communicate that best fit your communication style and needs.
2. **Use the Networlding Exchange Summary** tool to keep your interactions on target and substantive. It can be very easy to get off track with our conversations - this will help keep the relationship growing in the right direction. You will see a sample of this tool in your participant guide as well.
3. **Develop a list of your top three things to accomplish.** Within each conversation, stick to 3 things you want to accomplish for that call. Limiting it to 3 will force you to be strategic and intentional, plus give you a great sense of accomplishment.
4. **Set expectations from the start and for each conversation.** When expectations aren't clearly articulated, and both sides aren't buying in, it can stall the relationship. For example, take a look at the goal you set back in step 1. If that's your primary focus in the next 6 months, be clear about that and see where your potential Networlding partner stands. Do they want to work on your opportunity, or do they have other expectations/opportunities to address?
5. **Brainstorm.** Idea creation is so important to the Networlding process, so take time during a conversation or in another method that works for you (email for example) and make sure you're keeping the flow of ideas going.
6. **Share connections.** Introducing and being introduced to others leads to gratitude and respect - which help your relationships blossom. Think about a time someone introduced you to a great contact - how did you feel about the person who connected you? Ask these two questions of one another often: "Who do you know?" (open-ended) and "Do you know X?" (closed). Asking both increases the odds you'll cover all the people bases.
7. **Prepare for each conversation.** Preparation breeds confidence and shows your commitment to the Networlding partnership. Before each conversation, consider creating an agenda. Know what you want to share, what you want to accomplish and what information you need.

8. **Keep the discussions current.** Topical, timely exchanges fuel relationship growth. Don't focus on the past or old information - always strive to stay fresh. When you learn new information or make a new contact, make it a point to share quickly and often with your Networlding partners. This openness generates a greater number of quality opportunities.

9. **Overlap your circles.** Become highly aware of who is in your primary, secondary, and tertiary circles and share the names of these people with your Networlding partners (and vice versa). It's a sign of generosity and trust to open your circles to one another.

10. **Create action steps.** All talk and no action will lead you in circles rather than to a set goal. In each interaction, be sure to create at least one meaningful action step that each person will accomplish and commit to it. And in between conversations, lend support following the support exchange model. What emotional, information, knowledge, or promotional support can you offer each other to achieve your action steps?

11. **Summarize and set the next conversation.** This seems pretty obvious, but it's often overlooked. Summarize the key points from the exchange and determine when you will meet next. If you don't do this, it's easy to let the things of life get in the way and unintentionally stall the relationship and your goals.

SCRIPT: We've covered a lot of ideas here, between your contributions and the Networlding content. Are there any questions, comments, or experiences, you would like to share before we move on?

LESSON 2 - COMMUNICATE ON A MORE MEANINGFUL LEVEL

(15-20 minutes)

SCRIPT: In lesson 1 we talked about some tactical ways to maximize your interactions with Networlding partners. In this lesson we're going to discuss the internal work of communicating on a more meaningful level with others. We will discuss:

1. Understanding communication styles
2. Keeping an optimistic outlook
3. Listening actively
4. Being here now
5. Communication equally
6. Staying connected

Each action leads to enjoying equal opportunities in the relationship.

There is space in your participant guide to take notes and jot down ideas for your own Networlding partners.

Let's first talk about **communication styles (1)**.

We touched briefly on it in the previous step. Some people are talkers who enjoy pontificating; others are listeners who love to hear others speak. There are people who quickly get to a point and can't stand it when others don't do the same. Ideally you're aware of one other's styles and adapt accordingly.

Within communication styles, we have to pay attention to the other person's language and adopting it. This is also known as "mirroring," and that was discussed in step 4 as well. Mirroring helps facilitate consensus and understanding, shows we have sensitivity to others, and that we're listening carefully.

For example, does the other person:

- Have a very business-like style or does he or she use more colloquialism?
- Use a lot of industry jargon?
- Speak with brevity, or is he or she long-winded?
- String lots of sentences together without pausing for input?

Being aware of these styles and adapting to them - while still being you - will help you establish a better bond.

Insight from Making Your Net *Work*
Chapter 9: The Art of Building Your Network.

Keeping an optimistic outlook (2) creates connection opportunities. I always set out with expectations that good things will happen. At my core, I'm an optimist. Doing the right thing by people always comes back as a blessing. I think you always have to see possibility! By taking ownership and having that expansive belief that anything is possible, you will realize the best possible opportunities. Take time to regularly envision all the opportunities that may come from your networks. Then like me, you will be prepared to leverage your opportunities into connection hubs.

Next, let's talk about **listening actively (3).**

Do you validate others by showing active, rather than passive, listening? In passive listening, you sit there and absorb, rather than respond. And the speaker may feel as though what he or she is saying is not impacting you - it may have a negative consequence.

On the other hand, if you're an active listener, you're truly trying to respond to and understand the other person. You're leaning forward, you're attentive. You might nod your head occasionally or ask a thoughtful question to show you're following along and really paying attention to the other person. You see the difference?

At its core, a successful networking process starts with listening. This can be face-to-face, or online. By listening with each of the people we meet when we're networking, we are able to find what matters to them, and from there, help them through our connections. Also our respective ideas for growing our careers or businesses move ahead faster. You can do the same. It's easy. What are your current networking partners interested in? What are their jobs? What do they do in their spare time? What is a fun day for them? Connecting with people is about being honestly interested in what makes them tick.

Insight from Making Your Net *Work*
Chapter 9: The Art of Building Your Network.

When I connect the concept of **being here now (4)** to networking, I *feel* my way through it. There's definitely the *science* side of networking—from the process side. The art side of networking is all about being real and authentic and open to possibilities. Being authentic in the moment helps me make deeper, more lasting connections.

Have you ever met someone new who races through their story, and all you hear is what they want? An authentic exchange happens only if they can let go of *telling* what they think we want to hear and start exploring for connection points instead. Take time to think and ask, "How can I be helpful to you?"

I would argue that success in networking comes down to more of the art than science side. This is where it gets scary for some folks. This deepness, this "professional intimacy" as I call it, is almost spiritual, or at least reverential. The reverence is the feeling part. We've slowed down and listened to one another. We've been vulnerable and real. Some folks back off this part of the process. For me, I don't compromise on the process.

Then there is also the issue of **communication equality (5).** What this means, is there an equal sharing of:
- Ideas and information
- Talking and listening
- Questions and commentary

If you feel that the communication is one-sided, it can start to cause friction in the relationship, so it needs to be addressed right away. But it doesn't need to be perfect - we're all different and bring different skills to the table. There will be times when someone may contribute lots of ideas, or ask lots of questions . . . what you're looking for is overall equality.

Finally, let's talk about how we **establish comfortable ways of staying connected (6).** For example, if you love to talk by phone, but your partner prefers email, you need to find some common ground. Make it a point to ask the people you're connecting with how they like to communicate, and make sure they know your preferred methods so you can decide together how best to accomplish it. It shows thoughtfulness and respect on your part.

So each of the examples we just talked about - communication styles, keeping an optimistic outlook, active listening, being here now, communication equality, and staying connected - all improve our chances of enjoying equal-opportunity relationships.

Insight from **Making Your Net *Work***
Chapter 11: Create a Robust Networking Strategy.

Also consider when to do one-on-one vs. group networking. In deciding between a one-on-one meeting versus a connecting-people meeting there are a few things I consider. What level of connection exists already? If there's not a strong connection already, I'm hesitant to bring other people into that. I want to build my one-on-one connections first.

Think about the location and its environment, too. Where I go is relaxing, casual, and calm. It inspires strong networking exchanges.
- **Consider where you're currently networking.** Is there a special go-to place you have where everybody knows your name, like at *Cheers*?
- **Remember to look for a quiet place where you can hear the other person**. If you have to raise your voice to talk, your conversation and connection may be compromised. Just suggest, "Why don't we step over here to a quieter spot where we can hear one another better?"

- **You have only one chance to make a first winning impression.** Make sure you have set yourself up for success with the space you choose to start and build great connections.

Although opportunities may be difficult to come by in the initiating stage of Networld relationships, they become more plentiful as relationships evolve. You and your partner become more comfortable with one another and more willing to extend your trust. The biggest difference I hope you see is that opportunity development becomes *conscious and intentional*, rather than *unconscious and reactive*.

So, how do we enjoy equal opportunity relationships? There are fill-in-the-blanks in your guide and space for notes while we discuss.

FACILITATOR NOTE: Point out the fill-in-the-blanks to the class.
1. Identify the opportunities
2. Exchange wisdom support
3. Build community
4. Be proactive

Let's talk about **identifying opportunities (1)**. First, always know that opportunities surround you and your Networlding partners. The trick is to flush them out into the open. Keep your horizon of observability in mind - that even though connections and possibilities are not immediately visible, they are there.

SCRIPT (CLASS DISCUSSION): So how do you begin to identify new opportunities within your reach?

FACILITATOR: Capture ideas from the class on a whiteboard or flip chart. Be prepared to share a story of how you identified a Networlding opportunity.

SCRIPT: Great ideas everyone. Let's talk about some other potential ideas.
1. Has there been a hot topic of discussion between you and your partner or others?
2. Are there articles or blogs you've recently read?
3. What about discussions on social media sites, like LinkedIn and Twitter?
4. Is there a wished-for dream or opportunity that just doesn't seem to be there?

STORY EXAMPLE (INSERT YOUR OWN): I began telling you a story back in step 4 about the person I met at an industry group who is now part of my primary circle. We were at breakfast one day, talking about women in business and business skills - joking about how we wished we had some type of class in college that taught us all the stuff we really needed to know about starting out in the business world. Things like networking, knowing how to interact with co-workers and management, professional development, personal finance, etc.

Well that joking sparked an idea for a live workshop, aimed at millennial women to teach them those exact skills. From there we started brainstorming potential influential people to help us accomplish this, content ideas, presenters, etc. We're still in the exploring stages of that opportunity, but it started by talking a hot topic or a wished-for opportunity!

So the first point was about identifying opportunities. The **second point is exchanging wisdom support (2).** You'll remember from the support exchange model that wisdom support follows promotional support.

SCRIPT (CLASS DISCUSSION): Can anyone describe for me the difference between knowledge and wisdom?

FACILITATOR NOTE: Allow the class to discuss their perceived differences between knowledge and wisdom before sharing from Networlding.

SCRIPT: Great input everyone. Knowledge can be seen as knowing facts and sharing our experience with others. Wisdom takes knowledge further by adding good judgment, common sense, and sense of spirit to what we know. Wisdom not only helps us make enlightened decisions, but to help others see a situation from a different light and maybe make a better decision for themselves.

Offering wisdom support can be a much tougher, and definitely deeper, exchange with someone because it might involve having to say things that others may not want to hear.

Does anyone have a story they would like to share that shows the difference between knowledge and wisdom?

FACILITATOR NOTE: You may want to have an example or story of wisdom support to share with the class.

The next step in creating equal opportunities is to **build community (3)**. As we become more connected, what we share affects more people.

As you decide where you will place your energies in relationships, realize that you don't have to work as hard as you think to make a powerful difference for your Networld partners and the many lives you will impact as your opportunities expand. This is the ultimate effect of effective Networlding. And because we live in a world community, it's not unlikely that some of your Networlding partners will live around the globe.

The fourth step is to **be proactive (4)**. As we've already talked about, networkers tend to be more reactive and as Networlders, we have to be proactive in how we relate to our Networlding partners. Recognize that if you take the initiative and do more than your fair share, you'll not only increase your chances of getting opportunities, but you will spur others to action.

SCRIPT (CLASS DISCUSSION): What are some ways you can be proactive in your Networlding relationships when it comes to opportunities?

FACILITATOR NOTE: Allow the class to discuss before sharing from Networlding.

SCRIPT: Great input everyone. Here are some other ideas on being proactive:

1. Consider one of your Networlding partner's goals and create a list of people you know that might be able to help them and ask your partner if he/she would like the referrals.
2. Anticipate needs rather than waiting to be asked.
3. Mark down opportunities as they occur to you. It might be a job opening, a project, or connection.
4. Communicate potential opportunities regularly. They may not always turn into something, but just that simple communication shows that you're aware of what's important to your partners.

EXERCISE 2 - MEANINGFUL COMMUNICATION ROLE PLAY

(15 minutes)

SCRIPT: In this lesson we talked about how meaningful communication and how it plays a critical role in growing and nurturing relationships, and identifying the right opportunities for Networlding partners.

In this activity, we're going to create a role play around meaningful communication, so you can prepare for it in real-life exchanges.

FACILITATOR NOTE: An example situation is provided, but you may alter it or add others based on your audience's situation. <u>Both the directions and example situation are in the participant guide so they can follow along.</u>

DIRECTIONS FOR FACILITATOR: Have the class divide into groups of 4-6 people. Read the following directions to the class.

1. Your group is going to read the example situation, and create a role play. The example is generic, so please draw on your own experiences and add your own insights and details to the situation.
2. The goal of your role play is to reflect the different meaningful communication elements we discussed in lesson 2. But, feel free to add elements from lesson 1 as you see fit. It's up to you whether you show the good side or the not-so-good side of communication.
3. We'll take the next 5-7 minutes to create the role play, and then we'll have each group present.
4. Have fun with this!

EXAMPLE SITUATION FOR ROLE PLAY: One of you (choose which person) has identified potential Networlding partners through various situations, such as a live networking event, LinkedIn, and a trusted referral source.

You've talked with each one several times individually and have exchanged emotional, informational, and knowledge support with them, so there is some level of trust.

You have a goal you would like to reach in the next year, and you've decided to bring these individuals together in an in-person meeting because you think they might be a good fit for your primary circle and to bring the opportunity to reality.

They know of one another through you, and there have been some basic email introductions, but overall you're all still in the initial support exchange stages.

Applying what you now know about creating more meaningful communication, design a short role play that shows:

- Communication styles
- Passive and active listening
- Communication equality
- Staying connected

You may also choose to incorporate elements of lesson 1 into your role play as well.

FACILITATOR NOTE: Once 5-7 minutes has passed, bring the class together and ask several groups to present their role play. In between each role play use the debrief script below.

Debrief (script): Great job everyone! In the role play:

- What meaningful communication did you observe?
- Was there any negative communication you observed?
- How did the group (or did the group) establish trust?
- Overall, do you think the exchange was maximized to its potential?
- What did you learn that you could apply to your real-life exchanges?

CLOSING DISCUSSION: Ask for any additional questions, comments, or takeaways that the class has uncovered before moving on to step 6. You may also summarize the main points.

SUPPLEMENT - NETWORKING EXCHANGE SUMMARY TOOL

SCRIPT: This tool is in your participant guide. Use it to help you capitalize on interactions with your primary circle.

Networlding Partner	Meeting Information
Name:	Today's date/time:
Title:	Last meeting date/time:
Company Name:	Next meeting date/time:
Telephone:	
Website:	
Section 1: Referral Log of Names (Name, Contact Information, Nature of Referral)	
Section 2: Project Collaborations	
Section 3: To Do (Prioritize)	
1.	
2.	
3.	
4.	
5.	
Section 4: "Who Do You Know" or "Do You Know"	

STEP 6 - CO-CREATE OPPORTUNITIES

The sixth step in Networlding moves into opportunity creation. Creating opportunities together means that two Networlding partners expand their Networlding to new levels by leveraging their combined talent. Joint opportunities are more likely to occur as the relationship reaches maturity.

For this segment, you may want a flip chart or whiteboard. Participants have a corresponding guide to follow along. Take time to familiarize yourself with the participant guide.

AGENDA

Customize the agenda timing as needed.

TIME	ACTION	OBJECTIVE
5 minutes	Introduction	Communicate overall objectives
20 -30 minutes	**Lesson 1**: Co-Creation is the Networlding Way	Identify the ten guidelines for co-creating opportunities.
20 minutes	**Exercise 1**: Co-Creation in Action	Practice the guidelines for co-creation by brainstorming and on a participant's goal or idea.
15 minutes	**Lesson 2**: Behaviors for Co-Creation Success	Identify the opportunistic behaviors co-creation success.

OBJECTIVES

- Identify co-creation and its value to Networlding
- Discover ten guidelines for acting on joint opportunities
- Identify opportunistic behaviors in Networlding interactions

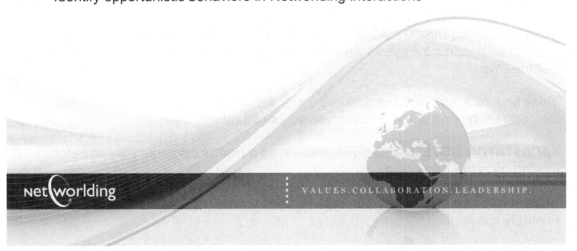

net(worlding   VALUES.COLLABORATION.LEADERSHIP.

LESSON 1 - CO-CREATION IS THE NETWORLDING WAY

(20-30 minutes)

SCRIPT: The Networlding process has hopefully helped you develop a deeper understanding of the value of quality relationships. When we choose the Networlding way to connect with others, those relationships enrich our lives and lead to transformational opportunities.

How can you best create transformational opportunities? Sometimes you're so focused on your day-to-day obligations that you fail to take the time to create, or co-create with your Networlding partners, opportunities that could benefit you and your organization in powerful, unique ways.

You can achieve your goals much faster if you use your Networlding partnerships as brain trusts. In addition, your partners can help you find things you didn't know existed, and enable you to avoid roadblocks and obstacles to success.

SCRIPT (CLASS DISCUSSION): Let's first talk about two terms, "co-create" and "transformational opportunity."

FACILITATOR NOTE: Capture answers on a whiteboard or flip chart.
- What does the term "co-create" mean to you?
- Now what does the term "transformational opportunity" mean to you?

SCRIPT: Great input everyone. Co-creating opportunities means that two Networlding partners expand their Networlding to new levels by leveraging their combined talent. As your relationships mature with your Networlding partners, co-creating becomes a natural extension of your relationships. Think of co-creating as moving from talk to action!

We don't initiate Networlding relationships just for the sake of it. At the heart of Networlding is the creation of transformational opportunities. These are opportunities that can truly change your career, your business, your community, or even your life. They speak to your heart rather than your head. You and your Networlding partners listen to one another; you understand what matters most, what stirs your passions - and as a result, expand that horizon of observability - creating opportunities beyond what you thought possible.

SCRIPT (CLASS DISCUSSION): We've probably all participated to some extent in co-creating an opportunity, even if we called it something else, or we weren't really aware of it at the time.

Think back to a successful opportunity you created with others are there any traits about the opportunity itself or the people involved that stood out to you?

FACILITATOR NOTE: Discuss this question as a class for a minute or two before moving on to the following guidelines.

SCRIPT: No matter how or where opportunities are co-created, the process remains relatively constant.

Let's look at the ten guidelines Networlders use to find and act on these opportunities.

There is space in your participant guide to fill these in and take notes.

FACILITATOR NOTE: As you review these guidelines, ask the class for any stories or examples that illustrate them. Be prepared to share a story or two of your own.

1. **Analyze complementary strengths.** Creativity springs from our differences - not in values or goals, but in skills, knowledge, and experiences. You listed your top strengths way back in step 1. Sit down with your Networlding partner and get to know his or strengths.

   One thing to look out for - if you're both talented or skilled in the same areas this could be problematic as you co-create opportunities. Why? You could risk duplicating one another, or not pushing each other in new directions. It's something to be aware of - you may need to bring in a third partner with a complementary strength.

2. **Share intentions.** This can be a tough one for people. Why? Because we sometimes operate from fear. Fear of sharing too much about ourselves; fear of people "stealing" our ideas; fear that someone will tear down their idea and rob them of the energy they need to make it happen.

   Sharing our intentions is an act of faith; we have to trust that our Networlding partners will respond in kind - and that we are honest, constructive, and fair with one another. When you openly share your intentions, it sparks dialogue - it can enhance your idea and lead to other, better ideas.

3. **Articulate and analyze opportunities.** Networlders aren't shy about examining opportunities from all angles - this is how they co-create the best possible scenario. This involves a significant amount of openness, and a lack of defensiveness.

   There are some key questions Networlders ask of one another to help improve the odds of coming up with a joint opportunity. Those questions are listed for you in your guide.
   a. What one opportunity do we hope to develop within the next 3 months?
   b. How does the opportunity reflect our values and strengths?
   c. How does it help us achieve our goals?
   d. What types of resources do we need to take full advantage of the opportunity?
   e. Who are all the people or organizations that could be involved with the opportunity?
   f. What first steps do we need to take to initiate the opportunity?
   g. Who else in our Networld might prove to be of assistance?
   h. What roadblocks might hamper this opportunity from developing; what creative solutions can we devise to address them?

4. **Practice reciprocity.** This might seem obvious, but reciprocity often becomes lost when an individual single-mindedly focuses on an opportunity. Without reciprocity, Networlding relationships collapse and resentment is created.

There are times when an opportunity benefits each Networlding partner equally, and reciprocity is a given. But there will also be times when one person may benefit more than the other from an opportunity. In those cases, the one experiencing greater benefit needs to make every effort to help the other with a project in the future. Examine cross-selling possibilities.

5. **Examine cross-selling possibilities.** An opportunity isn't simply a present "deal" between two partners; Networlders look to extend an opportunity to others. This isn't natural for most people. A hoarding mentality - based on a fear that someone will get more than we are getting - is common. When it comes to sharing clients and referrals, it can generate a lot of negative emotions. Networlders recognize this fear and make every attempt to openly discuss that issue.

6. **Form strategic alliances.** Who should you partner with? Should you be purely opportunistic and partner with the person who is in the best position to develop a specific opportunity? Does it matter if the person is in your primary, secondary, or tertiary circle?

   As a general rule of thumb, it makes sense to concentrate on co-creating with people in your primary circle. They're the ones who have the influence and shared values you need to produce a positive collaborative effort. But realize that not everyone in your primary circle will lead you to the types of opportunities you're looking for at a given time in your life.

   One person may help you achieve specific goals better than another - this is why you want to create strategic alliances. These are relationships you form to focus on targeted opportunities. They are strategic in the sense that they're planned - with long-term and short-term goals in mind, as well as the resources, tactics, and other elements needed.

   Here are some questions to help you determine if co-creating with a given person will result in a strategic alliance. These questions are also in your guide:
   a. Does the person share your goals in creating opportunities? What is motivating the other person, and does this match your motivation?
   b. Are the other person's strengths complementary or redundant to your own? Are they relevant to the type of opportunity you're pursuing?
   c. Does your prospective co-creator have the influence necessary to help you achieve your opportunity objectives, and is that person willing to use his/her influence?
   d. If this individual won't benefit as much as you will from this opportunity, are you in a position to help her achieve her goals for opportunities that are more beneficial to her?
   e. If you look at your Networld and your prospective co-creator's Networld, is there enough reach to the people and resources necessary to achieve your opportunity goals?

7. **Create mentoring opportunities.** Networlders create opportunities in all sorts of ways, and one very important way is mentoring. Think of the people who have

mentored you in your endeavors, many times for no financial gain, just the reward of helping you and learning from you. Networlders know the value of mentoring and realize its value is a two-way street. Consider how you can incorporate mentoring in your opportunity creation, formal or informal.

8. **Bridge divergent Networlds.** Co-creating also means constantly locating new people with similar values from diverse backgrounds. This allows you access to more diverse opportunities. People tend to run in redundant circles, so what happens is they continue to connect with the same people over long periods of time, and sometimes never venturing beyond those connections. Bridging divergent Networlds is a conscious effort; it's one you have to make in order to expand your horizon of observability.

Networking is borderless. It has no walls, but many doors. My lens says "diversity first." I look to create a collaborative, mutually beneficial atmosphere that I think occurs best when there's a diverse group. By thinking diversely, you're able to happen upon opportunity faster and better.

FACILITATOR NOTE: You may ask the class for their ideas on ways to bridge Networlds before giving them these ideas. These ideas are in your participant guide as well.

- o **Join clubs, associations, or other groups** that are organized not by profession but by some interest that encourages diversity; think civic organizations, political committees, not-for-profit volunteer groups, etc.
- o **Ask others in your Networld if you can go with them** to a meeting, seminar, or conference where the people are from different professions, have different interests, or different ethnicity/culture from you.
- o **Connect with colleagues** who might provide you with an introduction to people who are significantly different from the people you typically associate with.
- o **Use joint opportunities** created with a Networlding partner as "recruiting" tools to bring in people with divergent skills and knowledge in pursuit of your common goal.
- o **Connect like-valued people and groups together.** This strategy is about you becoming the matchmaker. By being the connector you become that person everyone wants to know because you make things happen. You create opportunities because you brought the people together, so you stand out as someone others want to know. In turn, opportunities will come to you.
- o **Utilize LinkedIn's new feature that allows you to connect through three degrees of your network.** This is a separate page with the heading, "People You May Know." Don't forget to send a private note that shows you care.
- o **Be selective.** Don't just throw two people or groups together. Make sure there are leaders in each group who will work collaboratively for the good of both groups. Test out your artful merging of networks with a small event. Take your time building initial events that are small, manageable, and filled with those from our networks who gave your feedback as to how to improve the next time.
- o **Keep improving your smaller events until the bugs are worked out and you can scale them.** Stay with your networked alliance of both groups to the point they're running smoothly. In other words, be a good shepherd of each group. By staying connected with those whom you play the role of advisor

(this would be the case with those you mentor), you have the opportunity to make an even greater impact on their lives.

9. **Play with opportunities.** Rather than look at things in a businesslike and linear approach, be more adventurous! Don't ignore obvious opportunities at your fingertips, but always be aware for what's beyond the opportunity in front of you.

   FACILITATOR NOTE: You might ask the class in what ways they've played and explored ideas before sharing these ideas. These ideas are in your participant guide as well:
   a. Create variations on your idea theme. See how many different ways you can spin your idea - you'll be surprised with what you come up with!
   b. Identify someone else's opportunity to see how you might contribute. What are those in your Networlding circles doing where your knowledge and skills might help their project flourish?
   c. Use provocative, unexpected questions to push opportunities further. Ask, and then ask more. We're very quick to want or provide answers, and very slow to ask. The more questions you ask, the more creative you can be in discovering opportunities.

10. **Think peripherally.** This is a figurative "turning of the head." Our focus can become so singular that we don't see what's in our peripheral vision. We all have blind spots to opportunities.

    How do you solve that? Make it a habit to look beyond your daily routines, get out of your comfort zone. Divergent Networlds facilitate this because you are constantly exposed to new people and ideas.

    How can you adapt your interests, skills and knowledge, a product, or a service into a seemingly unrelated use?

EXERCISE 1 - CO-CREATION IN ACTION

(25-30 minutes)

SCRIPT: This is your opportunity to begin co-creation, right here, today.
You'll be putting your new knowledge of values, circle partners, the support exchange model, and relationship exchanges into practice.

DIRECTIONS FOR FACILITATOR: This activity can be done in table groups of 4-6 people. Allow 20 minutes for the activity; adapt this time as necessary for your needs.

Explain the following directions to the class:
1. You'll work at your tables in small groups (about 4-6 people).
2. Select one person from your table who would like their goal or idea to be the brainstorm subject for co-creation opportunities.
   Use as many of the ten guidelines as possible that apply to the goal or idea being discussed. Be adventurous and playful! When you use the principles of Networlding you can't go wrong. Other questions to consider:
   o   Who in your primary circle may be a possible Networlding partner?
   o   Who else in your Networld may be able to contribute to the idea's success?
   o   How can you start exchanges with your Networlding partner(s)?
   o   What obstacles do you see stopping you? And how can you overcome them?
   o   How will bringing this opportunity to fruition be transformational?
3. The end result is hopefully an expansion on the idea or goal in question, possible co-creation opportunities, and some next steps toward making it a reality.

DEBRIEF: At the 20-minute mark, bring the class back together. Allow 5-10 minutes for discussion. Select one table (or as many as time permits) to share what they discussed. Use the following questions to encourage discussion:
- How did the guidelines influence your discussion?
- What next steps can the person take (who shared their idea for the activity) to further their idea or goal?
- How is the Networlding co-creation process different from how you've approached opportunities in the past?

LESSON 2 - BEHAVIORS FOR CO-CREATION SUCCESS

(15 minutes)

SCRIPT: The ten guidelines we just learned facilitate the co-creation process. You're probably realizing that because each opportunity is unique, some guidelines may be used more in depth than others.

But there are some behaviors that apply to every co-creation opportunity. Practicing these behaviors will make a difference in the quantity and quality of your co-creation possibilities. Essentially this means saying and doing things that encourage others to co-create with you or lend support to the opportunities that you're targeting.

Here's a checklist for you. There are fill-in-the-blanks in your participant guide to follow along:

1. **Continuously share information about your abilities.** This isn't bragging or being self-centered, it's simply making your Networld aware of your skills and knowledge. They'll appreciate knowing this information when they have an opportunity or goal.
2. **Treat your primary circle partners the same way as prospects.** Be willing to share opportunities with your primary circle partner. Treat them as if they were your best prospects by communicating regularly, being respectful and honest.
3. **Ask for and capitalize on referrals from your primary circle partners.** Never underestimate your circle's ability to provide referrals - and also be willing to provide them as well. If there's an opportunity you want to create, invite your primary circle to participate in its creation and development.
4. **Assess the influence of your primary circle members with referrals.** When you're provided with a referral, take time find out the relationship between your circle partner and referral to gauge the influence factor. The higher the influence factor, the less work you will likely have to do in making the interaction one that will facilitate your opportunity.
5. **Meet and exceed the opportunity needs of your primary circle partners.** Be proactive; volunteer information and ideas when people in your Networld send out a call for assistance. If you meet your partners' needs, they will be much more willing to meet yours.
6. **Demonstrate energy and commitment.** Networlding requires energy and it demands continuous communication. Co-creating opportunities is something that high-energy people do. Keep your commitments once you make them; magic happens when a committed Networld co-creates opportunities!

CLOSING DISCUSSION: Ask for any additional questions, comments, or takeaways that the class has uncovered before moving on to step 7. You may also summarize the main points.

STEP 7 - RE-CREATE YOUR NETWORLD

Networlds and the relationships they hold, are dynamic rather that static. The seventh step is not the end of Networlding, but continuous monitoring, assessment, and reformulation of your Networld.

For this segment, you may want a flip chart or whiteboard. Participants have a corresponding guide to follow along. Familiarize yourself with the participant guide.

AGENDA

Customize the agenda timing as needed.

Time	Action	OBJECTIVE
5 minutes	Introduction	Communicate overall objectives
30 minutes	**Lesson 1:** A Checklist for Your Networld	Tools to manage a fluid Networld for maximum efficiency and results
15 minutes	**Exercise 1:** Your Action Plan	Create an actionable plan to help learners apply this new information right away in their relationships
20 minutes	**Exercise 2:** Your Commitment to the Process	Table conversation and personal action plan to keep the process moving forward

OBJECTIVES

- Discover key ways to monitor, reassess, and reformulate your Networld for maximum impact - for you, your connections, and your community
- Create your commitment to the process

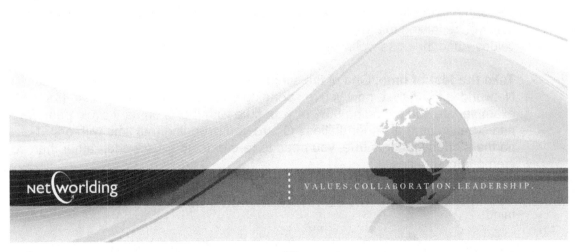

LESSON 1 - A CHECKLIST FOR YOUR NETWORLD

(30 minutes)

SCRIPT: I'd like for you to picture your Networlding circles for a moment. Think about your primary, secondary, and tertiary circles. Your circles are fluid - people are moving in and out of those circles as you create connections and opportunities. As you grow and change, so will your circles. It's a natural and important part of Networlding - your Networld is never static, always moving.

SCRIPT (CLASS DISCUSSION): Let's talk about some examples first.
- Can anyone share a story or example of a networking relationship that has changed?

FACILITATOR NOTE: Ask them to share why they think it changed and what they learned from the experience (this will tie into the checklist). Also, be prepared with a story of your own, especially if participants are having a difficult time coming up with one.

SCRIPT: Great input everyone. It's important to remember that relationships do change over time. People will move in and out of our circles. As Networlders, we need to remain aware of that and open to new connection and new opportunities.

With that in mind, this seventh step is about keeping on top of developments in your Networld and using this awareness to re-create it as needed - and your place in it.

FACILITATOR NOTE: Be prepared with a story or two for some of these checklist points, or ask the class to share as you review them.

Keep this checklist top of mind when evaluating your Networld. Fill in the blanks for this checklist in your participant guide.

1. **Reassess your goals, mission, and values.** Remember the house - you did this way back in step 1. But a lot of people don't take the time to do this, and it affects the quality of their relationships and results they achieve. There isn't a secret to knowing when a goal has stopped functioning for you, but it's a matter of measuring your passion for it.

   The same is true for your mission and values - tune into your instincts. Also, be sure you're talking to those in your primary circle about your goals, mission, and values - and theirs as well.

2. **Take the test of time.** One of the simplest and easiest ways to evaluate your Networld is to analyze how you're spending your time when you're in it. For example, are you spending 80% of your time with 4 or 5 primary circle partners and creating mutual opportunities? Or are you spending that time with only 1-2 partners? If the latter is true, you need to re-create your Networld, rather than co-create opportunities.

3. **Monitor and maintain the exchange dynamic.** To do this, keep three things in mind.

- o First, keep in touch by communicating with your primary circle at least once a month. Be proactive! Don't wait for someone else to initiate the contact.
- o Second, design a strategy (or several) to keep the exchanges evolving and meaningful. For example, create a short agenda of key items or questions - to keep your communication on target and mutually beneficial. If you trust that you have something to offer and are open to adding value and to giving, then you'll always be comfortable reaching out. That's a big chasm for some people when networking, especially young people. Once you integrate the principles of networking into your life, it becomes easier and less time consuming.
- o Lastly, evaluate what was exchanged. Were both of you satisfied with the exchange? Did anything fall short? Being honest about this will continually improve the quality of your exchanges.

Insight from **Making Your Net *Work***
Chapter 7: Your Brand Story

If a connection is made, and I know that I can be helpful, then I want to sustain that connection. It's just part of who I am and how I operate. I can always make time for a short phone call or a cup of coffee, especially if I know that the other person is looking forward to it. Even if I have no idea where this will lead or what the topic is, I know that during that thirty-minute conversation, I'll ask, "So how can I be helpful?" And if I can be helpful and the connection is made, I'll be there. If I can't be helpful, I will let them know and try to connect them with someone else to whom I can be helpful.

---

4. **Establish a comfortable work-life balance.** What happens when you become an established Networlder? You will have to deal with too many opportunities coming your way. It's easy to want to say yes to all of them, but part of the re-creating process is learning which opportunities to turn down. Evaluate each opportunity that presents itself in terms of your goals and values. Learn to say no (and this might be a process for you!) to those that don't fit. Keep this in mind: "You can tell the sign of a successful person by the number of times he or she can say no." It can be awkward at first . . . but you'll find with practice that you can do so gracefully and honestly - and you'll be respected for that.

5. **Continuously extend the connections.** It's easy to become comfortable with our immediate Networlding partners, but you always want to be looking to extend beyond that horizon of observability we've talked about.

   Two great questions to ask of your Networlding partners:
   - o Who have you enjoyed working with?
   - o And why? That first question helps you to identify individuals you could be introduced to (or introduce your partners to) and the second question helps match your interests, values, and goals that others may connect with. The key point here is to always remember there are so many connections beyond the obvious.

6. **Be open to new types of opportunities.** It's easy to fall into an opportunity rut! That means we keep pursuing the same types of opportunities, instead of new

challenges. But, there is a tradeoff that takes place - with every opportunity you choose, another will be tabled, permanently or temporarily. So what do you do? Make sure your goals, mission, and values are clear - they will guide you to the right opportunities. Be intensely aware of what it is you really want to achieve in your life. Those choices become easier to make.

Step away from your everyday routine and reflect on your connections. Think about things like who you currently know who might be good people to introduce them to or resources that might benefit them. This time will help you build even deeper, long-lasting relationships while increasing a spirit of reciprocity to offer similar support to you.

7. **Keep a maintenance checklist.** The best Networlders know that they can't coast when they get to step 7! To keep things fresh and effective, your Networld needs a tune up every once in awhile. Use this easy maintenance checklist:
    o Once a month, list out your exchanges. Compare it to the Support Exchange model and determine those exchanges are helping you meet your goals.
    o Are your primary circle partners also your friends? Networlding isn't all business, so if your partners are not friends, that's a sign something is wrong.
    o Evaluate your primary and secondary circles once a quarter. Ask yourself, "Should this person remain in that circle?" Your Networld is fluid, so don't be afraid to move people in and out of those circles.
    o Are your Networlding partners satisfied with the support and opportunities you're giving them? Encourage your partners to be honest with you about their satisfaction with the relationship - because if they aren't, you're likely to see less and less support on their part.

8. **Position (or reposition) yourself as a resource.** Don't assume that everyone knows what you have to offer. People often forget (or are unaware) of your talents and skills. With that in mind, graciously keep your primary circle members up-to-date on your projects and professional development opportunities. The Networlders who receive the most opportunities are those that regularly communicate and are known as resource providers.

A technique for gaining visibility and credibility is to write or email editors of periodicals. Contact reporters who write about your field and offer yourself as a resource for additional articles. Whatever you can do to make a reporter's job easier is usually greatly appreciated.

Insight from **Making Your Net *Work***
Chapter 5: Strategic Networking.

---

9. **Be ambitious about Net*Work*ing.** Create a networking plan, then work it. Keep going back to your plan to adapt it to the results you're getting. Include your strategies for Net*Work*ing into your marketing plan. As you become more accurate at projecting, you'll build skills in visualizing and implementing. Integrate a social media strategy calendar in your plan so you continue to expand your presence on the web. Set realistic goals. If your goals are not realistic, they're just dreams, not goals. They should be aggressive enough for you to feel a sense of accomplishment by achieving them, but not unrealistic. A goal should be a challenge, not a chore.

Here's a quick activity for you: jot down 3-5 influential people in your industry that you would like to meet.

FACILITATOR NOTE: Allow a minute or two for this. Now that you've done that, communicate that list to everyone in your primary circle. Now you may not get a direct connection right away, but putting it out there lets others know, and that awareness can eventually begin to generate a pathway to a connection.

10. **Know when a relationship should end.** This one can be particularly difficult because we don't want to hurt feelings or burn bridges. But there will be times when relationships will need to end, for whatever the reason. There isn't a formula to follow, but be aware of a few things:
    o Have you or your partner shifted goals? This makes it very difficult to create joint opportunities.
    o Did your partner's values change (or possibly come to light)? You may discover you don't share the same values - what's important to you isn't as important to your partner as you initially thought.
    o Is there a lack of reciprocity? You discover your partner is more of a taker, rather than an exchanger and this creates an issue.

Listen to your instincts! And be honest and sensitive when you discuss this with your partner. It may be an issue that can be cleared up quickly, or it could be something deeper. Focus on the positives, do your best to not dwell on the negatives and create a rift. Also, remain open to a future reconnection!

11. **Develop Networlding savvy and maturity.** This will come with time and practice, but there are few techniques that can help accelerate your savvy and maturity in the process:
    o <u>Provide post-referral feedback</u>. When someone makes a referral for you, be sure to let them know the results. It shows your appreciation for the other person's efforts, and increases your odds of obtaining future referrals.
    o <u>Don't push a relationship</u>. There's a difference between proactive and assertive . . . and pushy. Networlders aren't pushy. For example, it's not pushy to ask for a referral; it is pushy to ask over and over again. Put

yourself in your partner's shoes, read their body language, or gauge their tone of voice. You'll see the difference in how people become more open to you.

o   Keep confidences. When you are known as someone who is reliable and able to keep something in confidence, you will become a magnet for information! As you re-create your Networld, information is your most valuable asset.

o   Learn to delegate. As you build a stronger and stronger Networld, the demands on your time will increase. You will have to prioritize what you will do and what to delegate.

o   Slow down to speed up. We move at the speed of light sometimes, and our relationships can suffer for it. A savvy, mature Networlder take a deep breath and reflects before moving forward on a connection or opportunity. Choose carefully, and you increase the odds of choosing correctly! This process may take you a bit longer, but you will be rewarded with reaching your destination that much faster because you chose correctly the first time.

o   Repair relationships. Point #10 talks about ending relationships. But a savvy and mature Networlder never does this prematurely. Recreating your Networld makes waves, and sometimes people aren't ready for those waves. So, when a rift does occur, use it as an opportunity for open, honest communication. Attempt to repair any breaks in the relationships where it makes sense.

Insight from Making Your Net *Work*
Chapter 14: Integrate Networking into Your Everyday Life

If you're looking at creating and sustaining vibrant networks, you have to truly understand the value equation. When you do that, you can merge networking into your life and create a seamless integration. But if you're out there doing ad-hoc networking, thinking something like, "maybe I'll go there and try that"—which is the way many people network incorrectly—you won't reach sustainability. That's where the big value and payoff is. It's not about the number of people in your network. Remember, as we said earlier, it's about the quality.

EXERCISE 1 - YOUR ACTION PLAN

(15 minutes)

SCRIPT: This is one of your last activities in the Networlding course, your action plan! The goal is to help you keep the momentum going and the learning fresh - so you can create your Networld once you leave here.

Ideally, you should fill this out once a month for consistency and results. There is an action plan in the Appendix at the end of your participant guide.

Insight from **Making Your Net *Work***
Chapter 11: Create a Robust Networking Strategy

Probably the best way to illustrate the concept of creating a networking plan with a timeline integrated into it is to give you an example. Every two years, Chicago United runs a business leadership conference. They identify forty-five minority business leaders—black, Hispanic, Asian—according to certain criteria. Candidates are nominated, complete an application, and then a review is conducted.

In 2003, they nominated the first class, and among those leaders was a young community organizer named Barack Obama. Michelle Obama attended the 2005 class.

Billy Dexter was nominated in 2007 but wasn't selected. He set a goal to become a business leader of color. He didn't know Gloria, Chicago United's Executive Director, at the time, so he asked his friend, Roger, to introduce him to Gloria.

In 2009, several partners, including the CEO of Billy's company Heidrick, nominated him. That year, Billy was selected as a "business leader of color." By 2015, one of the people Billy nominated, Roger, was the person who had introduced me to Gloria, so it all came full circle. And at least two other people nominated by Billy were also inducted.

What's even more amazing? Billy subsequently was asked to host and chair the selection committee. Consider that in 2006, he didn't even make the list. Then in 2009, he made the list, and now he's the one making the list. It's an incredible full circle moment.

That timeline shows you have to be patient, have a plan and be persistent. Understand the power of time. If you march confidently in the direction of your dreams, you'll be met with greatness.

DIRECTIONS FOR FACILITATOR: Ask the class to take the next 10-12 minutes (individually) to begin filling in their action plan. They won't complete it in the allotted time, but the idea is get them started so they can finish on their own.

On the following pages is a copy of the action plan they will see in their guide.

DEBRIEF: At the 10-12-minute mark, ask the participants to wrap up their action plan and remind them to complete them on their own. Make the following points about the action plan:

1. It is designed to be incorporated on a monthly basis so you can track your progress and relationship building.
2. You can also see at a high level where you need to make improvements, and the positive impact you're having by co-creating opportunities with the right people in the right way.
3. It works best when your primary circle partners use it as well!

SUPPLEMENT - YOUR ACTION PLAN

Month:	
What are the results I have achieved to date on my goal?	
Changes to goal (if applicable):	
What top benefits have I received from my primary circle partners this month?	
What top benefits have I offered my primary circle partners this month?	

Partners supported:	What did I give?
	What did I receive?

Great organizations or trade shows I have attended:	Details of the event and top people to follow up with:

net worlding

VALUES.COLLABORATION.LEADERSHIP.

Organizations I plan to join:	Special committees, events, or people to connect with:
Great referrals I have received:	Contact details, context of referral, and conversation starter suggestions
Great potential primary circle partners:	Scheduled meetings and conversations I will initiate:
Partners I will follow up with in the next month:	Ideas for support I can offer, ideas for support I can request:
Partners I plan to co-create opportunities within the next month:	Ideas and details:

net(worlding   VALUES.COLLABORATION.LEADERSHIP.

Top partnering story:	
Overall estimated financial results from connections:	Breakdown of results:
To do's:	Details:

Start a Networlding Circle and PASS IT ON. Networlding is about learning, growing, and most of all - sharing. If you share it, it will come back to you tenfold.

Net worlding

VALUES.COLLABORATION.LEADERSHIP.

EXERCISE 2 - YOUR COMMITMENT TO THE NET*WORK*ING PROCESS

(20 minutes)

SCRIPT: In this final activity, you'll have the chance to review your learning from the previous steps. Networlding works best when you add the best practices you've learned here to your collective knowledge base. And when you actively practice, you retain more information and hopefully utilize it in your daily interactions.

DIRECTIONS FOR FACILITATOR: Conduct this discussion activity at each table. There is space in the participant guide for notes. Allow 10-12 minutes for discussion.

Explain the following directions to the class:
1. You'll work at your tables.
2. Discuss the following questions at your table.
   o What are 2 key lessons you've learned in this process that will help you become a better Networlder?
   o What new or potential opportunities have you identified or created as a result of this course? These opportunities could be professional or personal.
   o What support can you provide your Networlding partners to help them achieve their goals, and what further support can you ask for in achieving your goals?

DEBRIEF: At the 12-minute mark, bring the class back together. Allow the next 8 minutes for discussion. Ask for volunteers to share these two pieces of information:
- What key lessons have you learned to help you become a better Networlder?
- What new opportunities have you identified or created as a result of this course?

FACILITATOR NOTE: You may wish to close with a final review of each of the steps in the Networlding process. Encourage the class to support one another in the Networlding process - you may even find they are doing this already!

Insight from **Making Your Net *Work***
Chapter 14: Integrate Networking into Your Everyday Life

The whole ideas behind being a network thinker is that you're always thinking about how you can connect others, add value, and help those who need help. This is something that you need to develop and then integrate into your lifestyle. By that, we mean that the process becomes such a part of you that you can't turn it off, even if you want to.

I've come to embrace my experience as a message I would like to pass on to others: "You can get there from here." This means that no matter where you started or are currently starting, you can get where you want to go. It's really up to you. There's a path, and you can get there. You can make powerful requests. You can pray, but it really comes down to you in the end. You can't turn true and caring networking on and off. Further, if you commit to the practice of this type of networking, it becomes part of your character, how you act, who you are. It's your life.

A final thing that has made my net *work* is something that outsiders have constantly remarked about: understanding the awareness that you walk in and out of networks every day. We referred to this earlier as being *awake in your network*. In other words, if you're vigilant, you'll see regular opportunities to make connections that create opportunities for yourself and others while, simultaneously, continuing to grow the strength of your network. Just as the people who buy from you most will be repeat buyers, those who refer opportunities to you will refer again.

Many of us have family commitments, we work ten to twelve hours a day, we may have frequent travel; things can get complex and challenging. From the outside, many people wonder how anyone can be a master networker with all of these commitments. However, it's less about the time required and more about the philosophy behind this commitment. It's about making the initial effort to integrate networking into your lifestyle.

Every item on your calendar and every decision you make about networking can be strategic and intentional. The networks where your invest my time should be those you're passionate about and have interests that you can share you're your friends and family.

Ultimately, over time, your time becomes a network of connected events, organizations, and people, all of which you walk in and out of every day. When you have interconnected your networks there will be days when you can touch five or six of them, whether by phone, online, or at events. It's the power of *integrating* your networks that will generate the most benefits daily for you.

Getting to that next level of networking, whether it's getting an introduction or meeting, or being invited to join a club or organization, or becoming a board member, takes a certain amount of strategy. It requires you to look at the landscape of your potential connections and assess where you are and where you want to be connected. Then connect your networking into your lifestyle.

You can create interconnected synergies and, as a result, more effectively leverage your networks. It starts with creating one significant relationship and then another, and then continuing, one connection at a time, to make introductions and offer support to those connections. This is giving on your part that will build stronger relationships. Then, as you combine your one-to-one networking to include participating and supporting other networks that can become connection hubs (like professional associations or social clubs), you'll see the benefits of your efforts.

No matter your experience, skill level, or degree, if you don't connect with people in business—if you don't figure out how to navigate and be a team player—you have nothing! That's true at all levels.

You don't have to charge up to the front of a group demanding to be a leader. If you are focused, hold firm to what you believe in, and are action-oriented, people will follow you.

A few final tips
- **Become a networking influencer.** You may not yet be at the top of your field, but because you're willing to practice influencing—connecting people who

haven't met but who should meet—you can quickly become a top influencer, creating many opportunities for yourself. For example, you might know people in your industry who are highly influential but are not good influencer partners because they keep their power to themselves or confine their power to a small, insular group of colleagues. Their influence is actually limited because they don't understand how to be inclusive and diverse with their networking.

- **Study and model the successful networkers.** Treat all people as potential partners in networking. Your short-term objectives will keep changing, whereas your long-term ones will remain stable. Looking back, I can see that Rich influenced me tremendously. I was learning to network without even knowing it.
- **Realize that networking effectively is about building long-term relationships, not just collecting names and numbers in a database.** What you can't give today, you'd be surprised to find you can give tomorrow. Your intent to deliver is what really matters. As a proactive networker you'll find that you can create opportunities for your referral sources as you build a circle of high quality, rather than high quantity relationships.
- **Create three top signature success stories.** These are your stories that pass on both tacit and explicit knowledge about who you are and why others should care. Use these stories to build credibility, but, more importantly, connection with your contacts. If you have trouble creating your own stories, ask a colleague to interview you and record the interview.

Whether you call it art or science or you have blended the two mindsets, it's all about making your net *work.* We hope that through this seminar you've found some ideas that you'll go out and try as early as tomorrow. Now, our greatest wish for you is this: pay what you've learned here *two-ward.* In other words, share your insights with at least two people. That way, you'll not only keep reaping the rewards of your knowledge, but also build a life that's meaningful and, most significantly, *make your* net *work!*

Here's to your ongoing success!

Excellent job everyone! As you'll learn, the real payoff for working and living in the Networlding universe goes far beyond the many opportunities you create with others.

The process gives you the chance to be successful and the chance to help others become successful. When you interact with people as a true Networlder, you not only reap professional rewards but also understand that you've made the world a better place for both the people you know and people in need.

CLOSING DISCUSSION: Ask for any additional questions, comments, or takeaways that the class has uncovered.

APPENDIX

Here is a list of tips from this course, with additional new tips as a bonus.

Insight from **Making Your Net *Work***, Appendix.

- **Start with what Melissa calls your "Power-of-Ten Circle."** This involves building one-to-one relationships with ten or fewer people. These are people who hold similar values to you. They are great choices as networking partners. This is what I've done with groups like my Circle of Friends golfing group.
- **Set up regular gatherings with your circles of support, either one-to-one or as a small group.** By building consistent exchanges with your networking partners and circles, you'll create more opportunities for yourself and others.
- **Make some of your connection events fun.** Whether it's a play, a sporting event, a concert, or just going out for a meal. It's the social side of networking that helps grow business opportunities. Even if you're just starting out, ask someone you admire to meet with you and perhaps even become your mentor.
- **Set up regular gatherings with your circles of support, either one-to-one or as a small group.** By building consistent exchanges with your networking partners and circles, you'll create more opportunities for yourself and others.
- **Make some of your connection events fun.** Whether it's a play, a sporting event, a concert, or just going out for a meal. It's the social side of networking that helps grow business opportunities. Even if you're just starting out, ask someone you admire to meet with you and perhaps even become your mentor.
- **Create one or two social media accounts.** If you don't have a LinkedIn, Google Plus, Facebook Business, or Twitter account, we highly encourage you to obtain at least one or two of these. Create robust profiles. In fact, LinkedIn, a professional network, say users with complete profiles are forty times more likely to receive opportunities through LinkedIn.
- **Start your own blog.** A general rule of thumb is that you should have at least ten posts addressing different subjects prior to sharing your blog in order to lend credibility to your effort. A blog enables your loyal friends and fans to consistently connect to you in a fresh and robust manner. Your blog should be your cornerstone for social networking, because it's of your own making and free of outside influences.
- **Join LinkedIn groups.** While you can join up to fifty groups, it's more practical to participate in six to eight groups and make your contributions meaningful. There are many topics to choose from and aligning yourself with your field of interest and industry should be easy. Ask insightful questions and provide informed perspective in discussions.
- **Don't become lazy about welcoming new followers online.** Interaction online is the name of the game. Take the time to look at your new follower's profile and ask them something about themselves or comment on something interesting you read about them in their profile. If you follow someone, do more than just ask to join their network. Take time to tell them why you want to join their page or group. Don't just settle for the standard, "I want to join your network" e-mail. Personalize your requests.

- **Follow up promptly after face-to-face meetings.** E-mail or call quality contacts you meet at networking gatherings promptly after an event to remind them of your initial meeting. You can even include your Twitter and LinkedIn when you reach out. Reserve Facebook for close personal contacts. Let them know you enjoyed meeting them. Focus on the appreciation you have for the original meeting and mention that you would like to stay connected. This is not a time to sell your services or products, but rather, a time to grow and deepen the connection around the relationship.

- **Stay in touch with your networking connections.** Build rapport and follow them on Twitter, connect on LinkedIn, and subscribe to their blogs. Maintain regular phone contact and e-mail with information of value such as upcoming events or groups or important industry happenings.

- **Grab a pen. Bring back the art of good written communication by writing thank you notes to all your old and new contacts.** Read trade journals in your industry. Find people who interest you and write to them using personalized note cards. Include an article you find online or in a magazine with a handwritten note at the top saying something like, "FYI, George. Thought you would benefit from reading this article! Warmly, Your Name"

- **Manage your networks using a tool such as Hootsuite, where you can integrate multiple accounts and schedule tweets and updates.** We understand you're busy, but avoid the temptation of utilizing automated "response" programs. If your participation in social media appears automated, your credibility will suffer. Provide for meaningful personal time in your daily schedule.

- **Curate content by choosing the best tweets, posts, articles, and other information (including your own best) and assembling it in one place.** Use a tool like Storify (which is especially good for interviews) and scoop.it (arranges it in a gorgeous magazine format). You'll be able to share them with your connections and establish yourself as a go-to person in your industry.

- **Network up and down.** When you network up you look for people who have influence in your industry or the community in general. These are the people with whom you can offer more connections of value as you meet people who they don't know but should know. Networking down is about being the mentor. Dave Ormesher, president of a great web-design and development company called closerlook, shared that he acquired a large account with a company because he had befriended and mentored one of their salespeople several years ago when everyone else would not give this person the time of day. Dave realizes that all people are worth the time it takes to let them know they're important and to provide them with guidance as to how to grow successfully.

- **Treat each person you meet with uncompromising respect.** Great networkers are zealots of respect and integrity. They're like the knights in King Arthur's roundtable. They care about creating relationships of honor.

- **Suspend judgment when you meet someone new.** We often find ourselves meeting people who, upon first glance, don't seem to have the wherewithal to exchange or just don't seem like the sharing type. However, we make it a rule to give each person the opportunity to exchange with us toward the possibility of partnership. I constantly mentor others toward becoming better partners. I see this as a way to teach the world through these people—how to be better at sharing. For instance, Melissa works with a journalist who was formerly homeless. Rather than focus on the "homeless" tag she looked past that, discovered the woman was a TED Global speaker and had connections at the top media outlets in the country. She was also a giver and a networker.

- **Be creative when thinking of people to contact.** Start with people who really like you and brainstorm with them. Get them to give you a few names of people they really like but for one reason or another you have never met.
- **Connect like-valued people and groups together.** This strategy is about you becoming the matchmaker. By being the connector you become that person everyone wants to know because you make things happen. It's people who create opportunities and because you brought the people together, you stand out as someone others want to know. In turn, opportunities will come to you.
- **Be selective. Don't just throw two people or groups together.** Make sure there are leaders in each group who will work collaboratively for the good of both groups.
- **Test out your artful merging of networks with a small event.** Through the years both Melissa and I have created events that have brought us ongoing new business opportunities. But we also took our time building the initial events that were small, manageable, and filled with those from our networks that gave us feedback as to how to improve the next time. We kept improving our smaller events until the bugs were worked out and we could scale them.
- **Stay with your formal networks to the point they're running smoothly**. In other words, be a good shepherd of each group.
- **Create a statement that tells others what you do in the most favorable way.** For example, an accountant might say, "I help people start and maintain small businesses by getting their financial business squared away."
- **Co- create opportunities that offer the biggest win for the greatest number of people.** Project collaborations, strategic alliances, and partnering opportunities are all examples of ways to leverage relationships for maximum gain.
- **Request a referral in one industry or company at a time.** People will more likely remember these types of requests. Why? Because they are more specific. Think about it. With as much information as we're bombarded with daily, it's hard for any of us to keep straight who asked us to help them let alone how we could best help them. This suggestion here of being more specific will go a long way help people remember your requests. Which leads to the next tip.
- **Become an active listener.** Listen for understanding versus listening for information. Your attention to your networking partner's needs and interests will help you create opportunities that can lead to even more and better opportunities for you in your networking exchanges.
- **Stay open to new ideas.** Appreciate the new information or different way of looking at things your network partners offer. Even if you don't agree with them, respect their opinions. Successful networking comes from being open to the different viewpoints and ideas others share.
- **Keep asking questions.** When you do the asking you can lead the conversation toward the most successful outcome and that outcome should be about both you and your networking partners gaining value from a networking exchange. Questions also keep both parties participating.
- **Create a list of the best questions for generating conversations.** Great questions set the stage for great answers. Great answers inspire. Think of the

best questions you can ask to start great conversation and exchanges. For example, if this were the best year of your life, what's the one thing you would do?

- **Stay genuine.** Being prepared is great, but without sincerity, you have nothing. When you're genuine and sincere, you'll attract people to you who naturally want to help you. Become interested in others. Find out what matters most to them and then center your conversations around their priorities. Of course, you should also share your priorities and network with those who care what matters to you as much as they care about what matters to them.

- **Become a networking influencer.** You may currently be someone who is not at the top of your field, but because you're willing to practice influencing—connecting people together who have not yet met but who should meet, in turn, you can quickly become a top influencer. For example, you might know people who are in your industry who are highly influential but are not good influencer partners because they keep their power to themselves or confine their power to a small insular group of colleagues. Their influence is actually limited because they don't understand how to be inclusive and diverse with their networking—something that would benefit them as well as others.

- **Study and model the successful networkers.** Treat all people as potential partners in networking. Your short-term objectives will keep changing whereas your long- term ones will remain stable.

- **Realize that networking effectively is more about building long-term relationships, not just collecting names and numbers in a database.** What you can't give to your network today, you would be surprised to find you can give tomorrow. *Your intent to deliver* is really what matters. As a proactive networker you'll find that you can create opportunities for your referral sources as you build a circle of high quality, not high quantity relationships.

- **Continue to spend quiet time, regularly, looking at the makeup of your network.** As you take time and look at your network, you'll discover links connecting from where you are now to goals and potential people who could help you achieve your goals.

- **Create three top brand stories.** These are your stories that pass on both tacit and explicit knowledge about who you are and why others should care. These stories can be about someone who has helped you, or how you have helped others, or about how you learned a new networking skill. No matter what, it's good to have a written account that showcases the value proposition you can bring to your network.

- **Use your stories to build credibility and connection with your network**. If you have trouble creating your own stories, ask a colleague to interview you and record the interview. If you want, pay them something for the effort, or treat them to lunch or dinner.

- **Create balanced networking exchanges.** Life's lessons keep bringing us back to this truth. You don't benefit in the end when you take much more than you give. Here, you often end up with much less that you would have received if you had been more generous. The same is true when you give much more than you take. Here you wind up with little to show for your efforts.

- **Become a Net*Work*er.** A Net*Work*er, unlike a networker, has ten or fewer key people whom they consider partners. These partners regularly exchange emotional support, information, knowledge, promotional support, as well as leads and referrals for new business or career opportunities. The focus of

NetWorking is on mutually beneficial exchanges with like-minded and like-valued people. The great thing about NetWorking partnerships is that they're fun and get results three to five times as fast as traditional networking relationships.

- **Spend 80 percent of your relationship-building time with your primary circle.** We know this is counter intuitive this focus will make all the difference in achieving better business opportunities, faster. Of course, that doesn't mean you can't have a large secondary or even tertiary network as evidenced on LinkedIn.
- **Consider where you're currently networking.** Is there a special go-to place you have where everybody knows your name, like Cheers?
- **Remember to look for a quiet place where you can hear the other person.** If you have to raise your voice to talk your conversation and connection may be compromised. Just suggest, "Why don't we step over here to a quieter spot where we can hear one another better?"
- **You have only one chance to make a first winning impression.** Make sure you have set yourself up for success with where you choose to start and show up as your best self.
- **Allow serendipities to happen.** People may come into your life for *a reason, a season, or a lifetime*, but you don't strategically say, "I'm going to go out and look for this person."
- **Look at your career in three-year increments.**
- This strategy helps you to stay more focused. You don't want to stay too comfortable. Decide whether you want to stay on for another three years or move on from your current place of employment.
- **Throw yourself a challenge.** Say you're good at marketing and sales. Explore groups where you focus on building other skills that are relevant. Here this may look like developing your technology skills.
- **Get visible.** For example, sit on a panel or volunteer for an in-house project that's not part of your daily workload or join a nonprofit.

FINAL NOTE

Script:

Billy and Melissa have included 12 months of our Making Your NetWork-Networlding Planner Sheets in the Participant Guidebook to help you network more effectively with your partners.

You can choose to make copies and give them to your networking partners or gift them their own copy of the participant guidebook to start their own networking circles of support and exchange.

Made in the USA
Las Vegas, NV
28 November 2023